U0900738

中华人民共和国
2024年国民经济和社会发展统计公报

STATISTICAL COMMUNIQUÉ OF THE PEOPLE'S REPUBLIC OF CHINA ON THE 2024 NATIONAL ECONOMIC AND SOCIAL DEVELOPMENT

国 家 统 计 局
National Bureau of Statistics of China

2025年2月28日
February 28, 2025

中国统计出版社
China Statistics Press

© 中国统计出版社有限公司 2025
版权所有。未经许可，本书的任何部分不得以任何方式在世界任何地区以任何文字翻印、拷贝、仿制或转载。

© 2025 China Statistics Press Co.,Ltd.
All rights reserved. No part of the publication may be reproduced or transmitted in any form or by any means, electronic or mechanical, including photocopying, recording, or any information storage and retrieval system, without written permission from the publisher.

图书在版编目（C I P）数据

中华人民共和国 2024 年国民经济和社会发展统计公报 = Statistical Communiqué of the People's Republic of China on the 2024 National Economic and Social Development : 汉英对照 / 国家统计局编 . -- 北京 : 中国统计出版社 , 2025. 3. -- ISBN 978-7-5230-0695-5

Ⅰ . F124-66

中国国家版本馆 CIP 数据核字第 2025GL1122 号

中华人民共和国 2024 年国民经济和社会发展统计公报

作　　者 / 国家统计局
责任编辑 / 郭　栋
装帧设计 / 黄　晨
出版发行 / 中国统计出版社有限公司
通信地址 / 北京市丰台区西三环南路甲 6 号　邮政编码 /100073
发行电话 / 邮购（010）63376909　书店（010）68783171
网　　址 / http://www.zgtjcbs.com/
印　　刷 / 北京捷迅佳彩印刷有限公司
经　　销 / 新华书店
开　　本 / 880mm×1230mm　1/16
字　　数 / 92 千字
印　　张 / 5.25
版　　别 / 2025 年 3 月第 1 版
版　　次 / 2025 年 3 月第 1 次印刷
定　　价 / 38.00 元

版权所有，侵权必究。
如有印装差错，请与发行部联系退换。

目 录

CONTENTS

中华人民共和国
2024 年国民经济和社会发展统计公报[1]

国家统计局
2025 年 2 月 28 日

2024年是中华人民共和国成立75周年，是实现“十四五”规划目标任务的关键一年。面对外部压力加大、内部困难增多的复杂严峻形势，在以习近平同志为核心的党中央坚强领导下，各地区各部门坚持以习近平新时代中国特色社会主义思想为指导，全面贯彻落实党的二十大和二十届二中、三中全会精神，按照党中央、国务院决策部署，坚持稳中求进工作总基调，完整准确全面贯彻新发展理念，加快构建新发展格局，着力推动高质量发展，全面深化改革开放，加大宏观调控力度，经济运行总体平稳、稳中有进，高质量发展扎实推进，新质生产力稳步发展，改革开放持续深化，重点领域风险化解有序有效，民生保障扎实有力，中国式现代化迈出新的坚实步伐。

一、综合

初步核算，全年国内生产总值[2]1349084亿元，比上年增长5.0%。其中，第一产业增加值91414

[1] 本公报中数据均为初步统计数。各项统计数据均未包括香港特别行政区、澳门特别行政区和台湾省。部分数据因四舍五入的原因，存在总计与分项合计不等的情况。

[2] 国内生产总值、三次产业及相关行业增加值、地区生产总值、人均国内生产总值和国民总收入绝对数按现价计算，增长速度按不变价格计算。根据第五次全国经济普查结果，并同步实施城镇居民自有住房服务核算方法改革，对国内生产总值、三次产业及相关行业增加值、全员劳动生产率等历史数据（包括图 1、图 2、图 3、图 9、图 10、图 11）进行了修订。

亿元，比上年增长3.5%；第二产业增加值492087亿元，增长5.3%；第三产业增加值765583亿元，增长5.0%。第一产业增加值占国内生产总值比重为6.8%，第二产业增加值比重为36.5%，第三产业增加值比重为56.7%。最终消费支出拉动国内生产总值增长2.2个百分点，资本形成总额拉动国内生产总值增长1.3个百分点，货物和服务净出口拉动国内生产总值增长1.5个百分点。分季度看，一季度国内生产总值同比增长5.3%，二季度增长4.7%，三季度增长4.6%，四季度增长5.4%。全年人均国内生产总值95749元，比上年增长5.1%。国民总收入[3]1339672亿元，比上年增长5.1%。全员劳动生产率[4]为173898元/人，比上年提高4.9%。

图1 2020-2024年国内生产总值及其增长速度

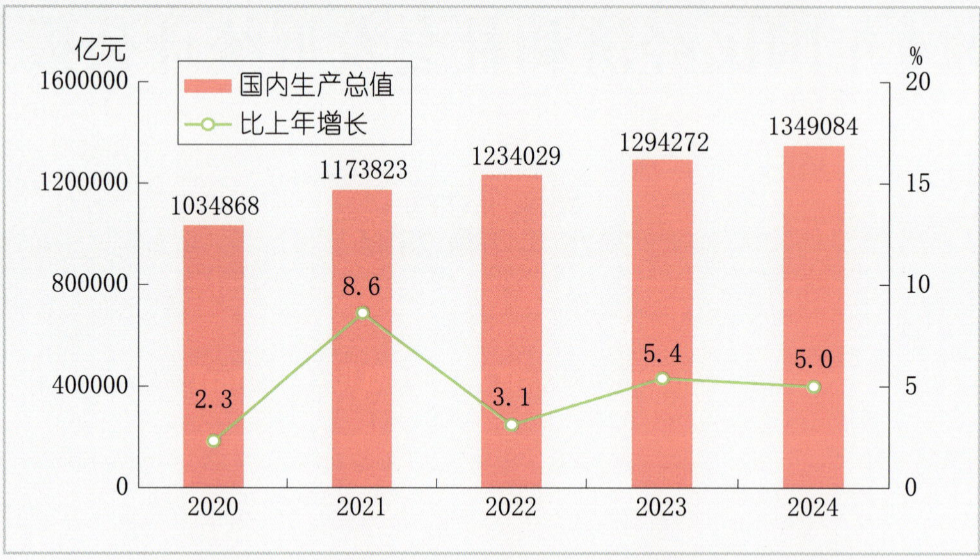

图2 2020-2024年三次产业增加值占国内生产总值比重

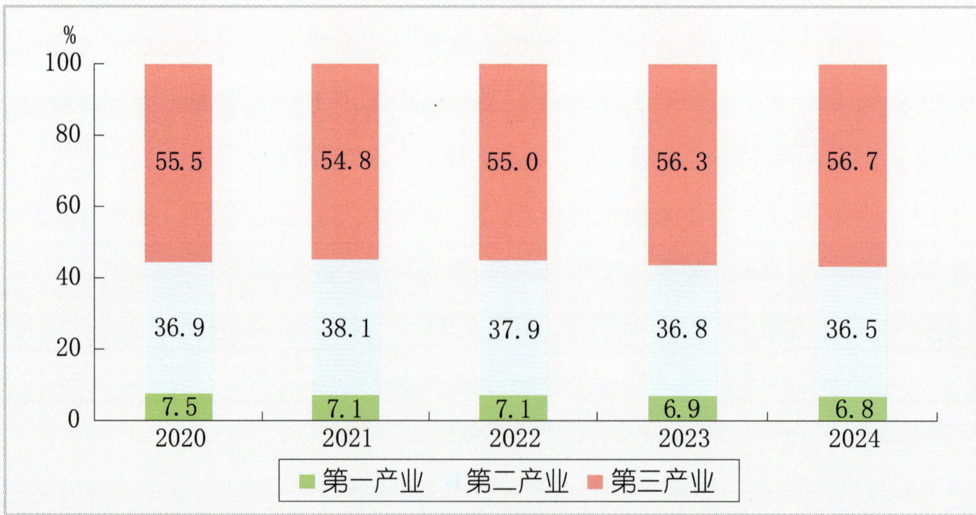

[3] 国民总收入，原称国民生产总值，是指一个国家或地区所有常住单位在一定时期内所获得的初次分配收入总额，等于国内生产总值加上来自国外的初次分配收入净额。

[4] 全员劳动生产率为国内生产总值（按2020年价格计算）与全部就业人员的比率。

图 3　2020-2024 年全员劳动生产率

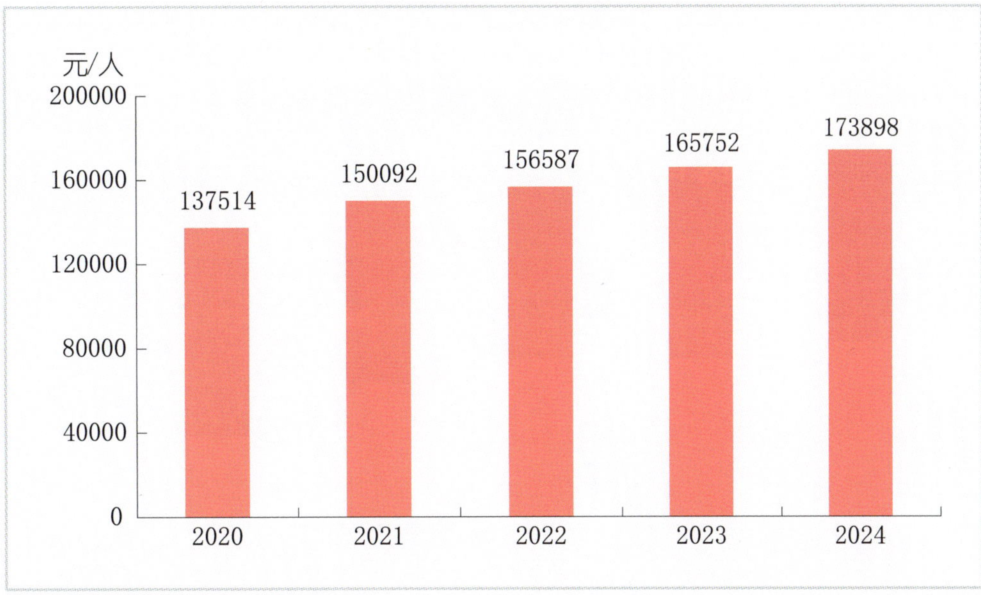

年末全国人口[5]140828万人，比上年末减少139万人，其中城镇常住人口94350万人。全年出生人口954万人，出生率为6.77‰；死亡人口1093万人，死亡率为7.76‰；自然增长率为-0.99‰。

表 1　2024 年年末人口数及其构成

指　标	年末数（万人）	比重（%）
全国人口	**140828**	**100.0**
其中：城镇	94350	67.0
乡村	46478	33.0
其中：男性	71909	51.1
女性	68919	48.9
其中：0-15 岁（含不满 16 周岁）[6]	23999	17.1
16-59 岁（含不满 60 周岁）	85798	60.9
60 周岁及以上	31031	22.0
其中：65 周岁及以上	22023	15.6

年末全国就业人员73439万人，其中城镇就业人员47345万人，占全国就业人员比重为64.5%。全年全国城镇新增就业[7]1256万人，比上年多增12万人。全年全国城镇调查失业率平均值为5.1%。

[5] 全国人口是指我国大陆 31 个省、自治区、直辖市和现役军人的人口，不包括居住在 31 个省、自治区、直辖市的港澳台居民和外籍人员。

[6] 2024 年年末，0—14 岁（含不满 15 周岁）人口为 22240 万人，15—59 岁（含不满 60 周岁）人口为 87557 万人。

[7] 城镇新增就业人数是指报告期内城镇累计新就业人员数与自然减员人数之差。

年末全国城镇调查失业率为5.1%。全国农民工[8]总量29973万人，比上年增长0.7%。其中，外出农民工17871万人，增长1.2%；本地农民工12102万人，增长0.1%。

图4 2020-2024年城镇新增就业人数

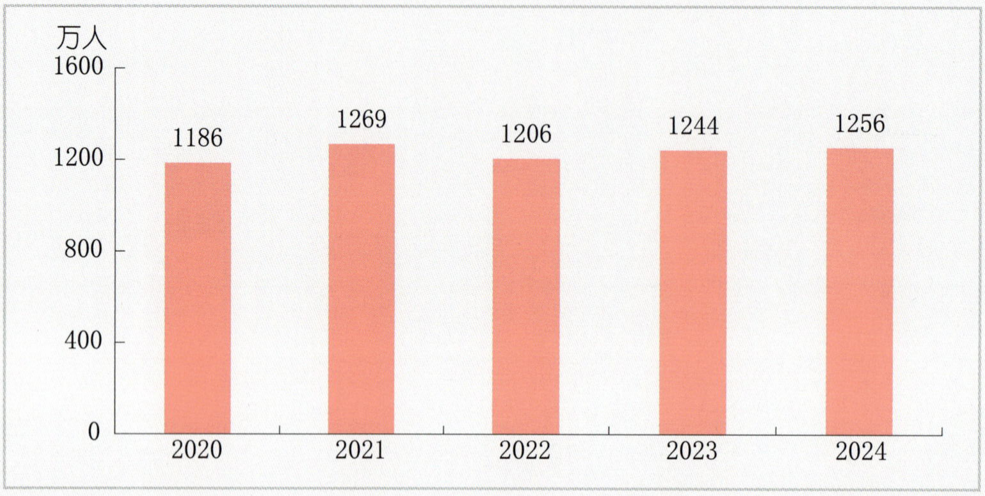

全年居民消费价格比上年上涨0.2%。工业生产者出厂价格下降2.2%。工业生产者购进价格下降2.2%。农产品生产者价格[9]下降0.9%。12月份，70个大中城市中，新建商品住宅销售价格环比上涨的城市个数为23个，持平的为4个，下降的为43个；二手住宅销售价格环比上涨的城市个数为9个，持平的为1个，下降的为60个；新建商品住宅销售价格同比上涨的城市个数为2个，下降的为68个；二手住宅销售价格同比下降的城市个数为70个。

图5 2024年居民消费价格月度涨跌幅度

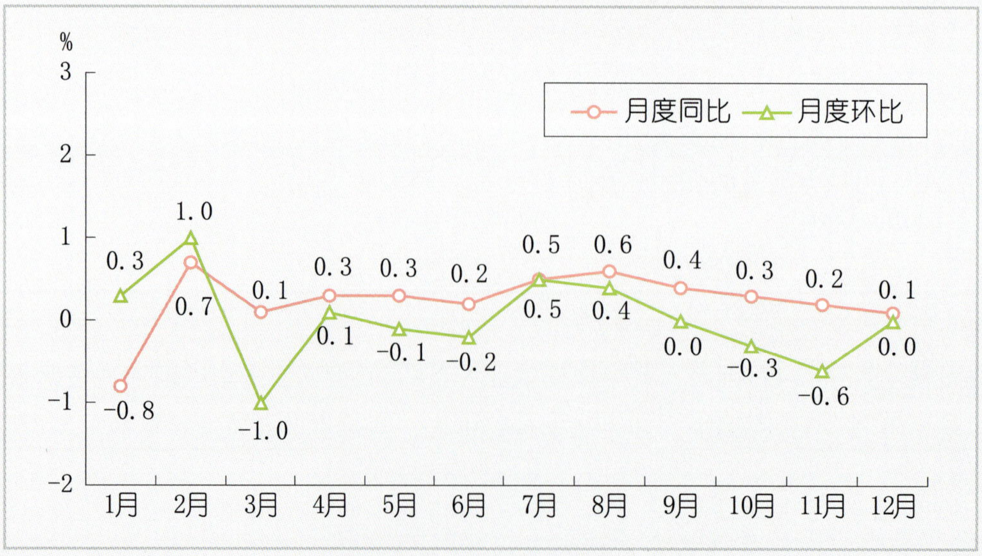

[8] 年度农民工数量包括年内在本乡镇以外从业6个月及以上的外出农民工和在本乡镇内从事非农产业6个月及以上的本地农民工。

[9] 农产品生产者价格是指农产品生产者第一手出售其产品时实际获得的单位产品价格。

表 2　2024 年居民消费价格比上年涨跌幅度

单位：%

指　标	全　国	城　市	农　村
居民消费价格	0.2	0.2	0.3
其中：食品烟酒	-0.1	-0.1	-0.1
衣着	1.4	1.6	0.9
居住[10]	0.1	0.1	0.1
生活用品及服务	0.5	0.4	0.8
交通通信	-1.9	-2.0	-1.5
教育文化娱乐	1.5	1.5	1.6
医疗保健	1.3	1.2	1.5
其他用品及服务	3.8	3.8	3.6

年末国家外汇储备32024亿美元，比上年末减少356亿美元。全年人民币平均汇率为1美元兑7.1217元人民币，比上年贬值1.1%。

图 6　2020-2024 年年末国家外汇储备

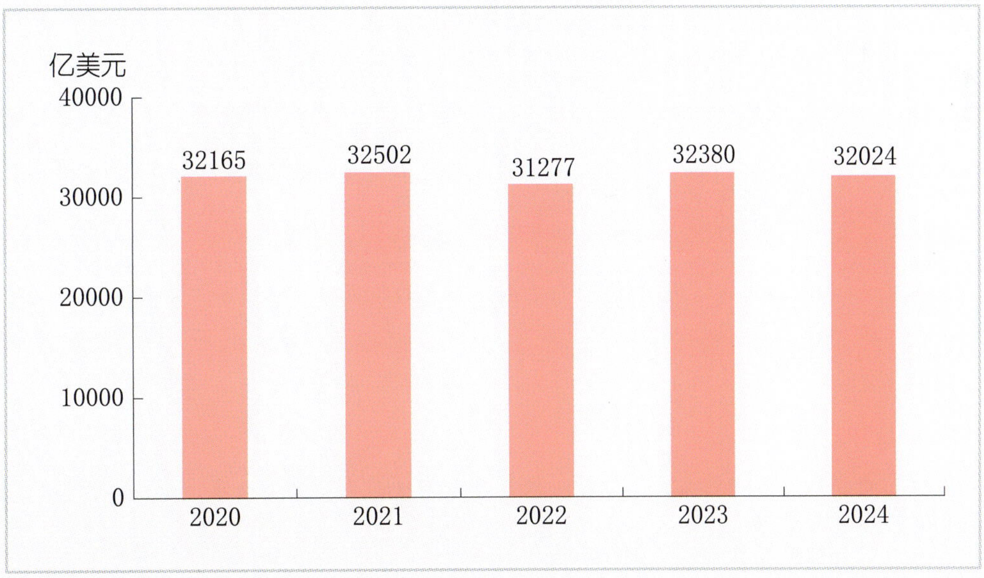

新质生产力稳步发展。全年规模以上工业[11]中，装备制造业[12]增加值比上年增长7.7%，占规

[10] 居住类价格包括租赁房房租、住房保养维修及管理、水电燃料、自有住房服务价格。

[11] 由于统计调查制度规定的调查范围变动、统计执法、剔除重复数据等因素，2024 年规模以上工业相关指标增速及变化按可比口径计算。

[12] 装备制造业包括金属制品业，通用设备制造业，专用设备制造业，汽车制造业，铁路、船舶、航空航天和其他运输设备制造业，电气机械和器材制造业，计算机、通信和其他电子设备制造业，仪器仪表制造业。

模以上工业增加值比重为34.6%；高技术制造业[13]增加值增长8.9%，占规模以上工业增加值比重为16.3%。新能源汽车产量1316.8万辆，比上年增长38.7%；太阳能电池（光伏电池）产量6.8亿千瓦，增长15.7%；服务机器人产量1051.9万套，增长15.6%；3D打印设备产量341.8万台，增长11.3%。规模以上服务业[14]中，战略性新兴服务业[15]企业营业收入比上年增长7.9%。高技术产业投资[16]比上年增长8.0%，制造业技术改造投资[17]增长8.0%。电子商务交易额[18]464091亿元，比上年增长3.9%。网上零售额[19]152287亿元，比上年增长7.2%。全年新设经营主体2737万户，日均新设企业2.4万户。

城乡融合和区域协调发展扎实推进。年末全国常住人口城镇化率为67.00%，比上年末提高0.84个百分点。分区域看[20]，全年东部地区生产总值702356亿元，比上年增长5.0%；中部地区生产总值287156亿元，增长5.0%；西部地区生产总值287350亿元，增长5.2%；东北地区生产总值63451亿元，增长4.4%。全年京津冀地区生产总值115394亿元，比上年增长5.2%；长江经济带地区生产总值630228亿元，增长5.4%；长三角地区生产总值331691亿元，增长5.5%。粤港澳大湾区建设、黄河流域生态保护和高质量发展等区域重大战略实施取得新成效。

---

[13] 高技术制造业包括医药制造业，航空、航天器及设备制造业，电子及通信设备制造业，计算机及办公设备制造业，医疗仪器设备及仪器仪表制造业，信息化学品制造业。

[14] 规模以上服务业统计范围包括：年营业收入2000万元及以上的交通运输、仓储和邮政业，信息传输、软件和信息技术服务业，水利、环境和公共设施管理业，卫生行业法人单位；年营业收入1000万元及以上的房地产业（不含房地产开发经营），租赁和商务服务业，科学研究和技术服务业，教育行业法人单位；以及年营业收入500万元及以上的居民服务、修理和其他服务业，文化、体育和娱乐业，社会工作行业法人单位。2024年规模以上服务业企业财务指标增速按可比口径计算。

[15] 战略性新兴服务业包括新一代信息技术产业、高端装备制造产业、新材料产业、生物产业、新能源汽车产业、新能源产业、节能环保产业和数字创意产业等八大产业中的服务业相关行业，以及新技术与创新创业等相关服务业。

[16] 高技术产业投资包括医药制造、航空航天器及设备制造等六大类高技术制造业投资和信息服务、电子商务服务等九大类高技术服务业投资。

[17] 制造业技术改造投资是指制造业企业采用新技术、新工艺、新设备、新材料对现有设施、工艺条件及生产服务等进行改造提升所完成的投资。

[18] 电子商务交易额是指通过电子商务交易平台（包括企业自建平台和第三方平台）实现的商品和服务交易额，包括对单位和对个人交易额。根据第五次全国经济普查结果，对电子商务交易额历史数据进行修订，2024年增速按可比口径计算。

[19] 网上零售额是指通过公共网络交易平台（主要从事实物商品交易的网上平台，包括自建网站和第三方平台）实现的商品和服务零售额。根据第五次全国经济普查结果对网上零售额和实物商品网上零售额数据进行修订，2024年增速按可比口径计算。

[20] 东部地区是指北京、天津、河北、上海、江苏、浙江、福建、山东、广东和海南10省（市）；中部地区是指山西、安徽、江西、河南、湖北和湖南6省；西部地区是指内蒙古、广西、重庆、四川、贵州、云南、西藏、陕西、甘肃、青海、宁夏和新疆12省（区、市）；东北地区是指辽宁、吉林和黑龙江3省。

图 7 2020-2024 年年末常住人口城镇化率

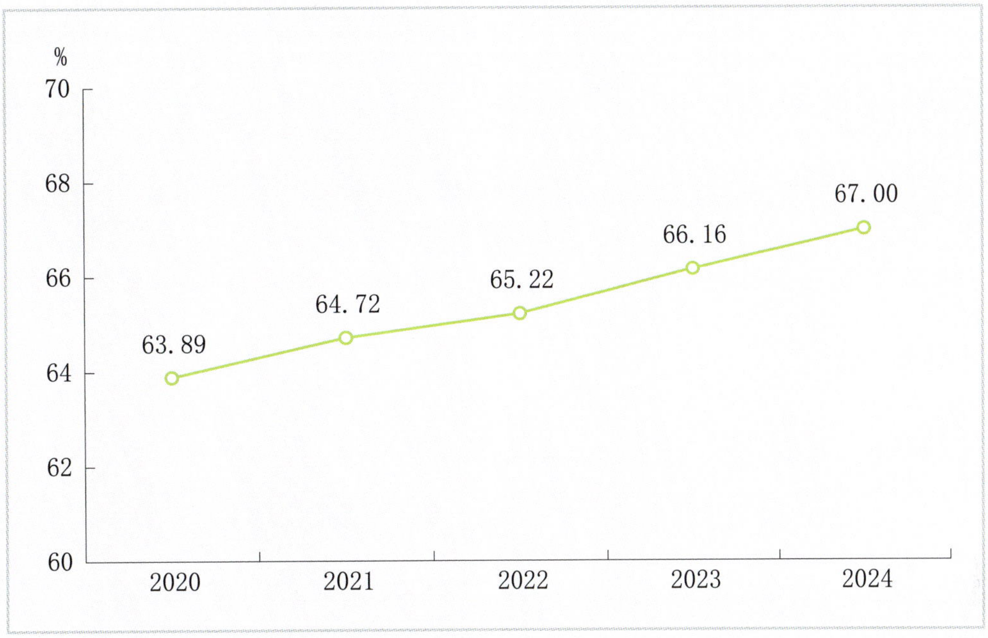

绿色低碳转型持续深入。初步测算，全年全国万元国内生产总值二氧化碳排放[21]比上年下降3.4%。水电、核电、风电、太阳能发电等清洁能源发电量37126亿千瓦时，比上年增长16.4%。在监测的339个地级及以上城市中，空气质量达标的城市占65.5%，未达标的城市占34.5%。3641个国家地表水考核断面中，水质优良（Ⅰ～Ⅲ类）断面比例为90.4%，Ⅳ类断面比例为7.8%，Ⅴ类断面比例为1.2%，劣Ⅴ类断面比例为0.6%。

二、农业

全年粮食播种面积11932万公顷，比上年增加35万公顷。其中，稻谷播种面积2901万公顷，增加6万公顷；小麦播种面积2359万公顷，减少4万公顷；玉米播种面积4474万公顷，增加52万公顷；大豆播种面积1033万公顷，减少15万公顷。棉花播种面积284万公顷，增加5万公顷。油料播种面积1429万公顷，增加37万公顷。糖料播种面积148万公顷，增加7万公顷。

全年粮食产量70650万吨，比上年增加1109万吨，增产1.6%。其中，夏粮产量14989万吨，增产2.6%；早稻产量2817万吨，减产0.6%；秋粮产量52843万吨，增产1.4%。谷物产量65229万吨，比上年增产1.7%。其中，稻谷产量20753万吨，增产0.5%；小麦产量14010万吨，增产2.6%；玉米产量29492万吨，增产2.1%。大豆产量2065万吨，比上年减产0.9%。

[21] 万元国内生产总值二氧化碳排放按 2020 年价格计算。

图8 2020-2024年粮食产量

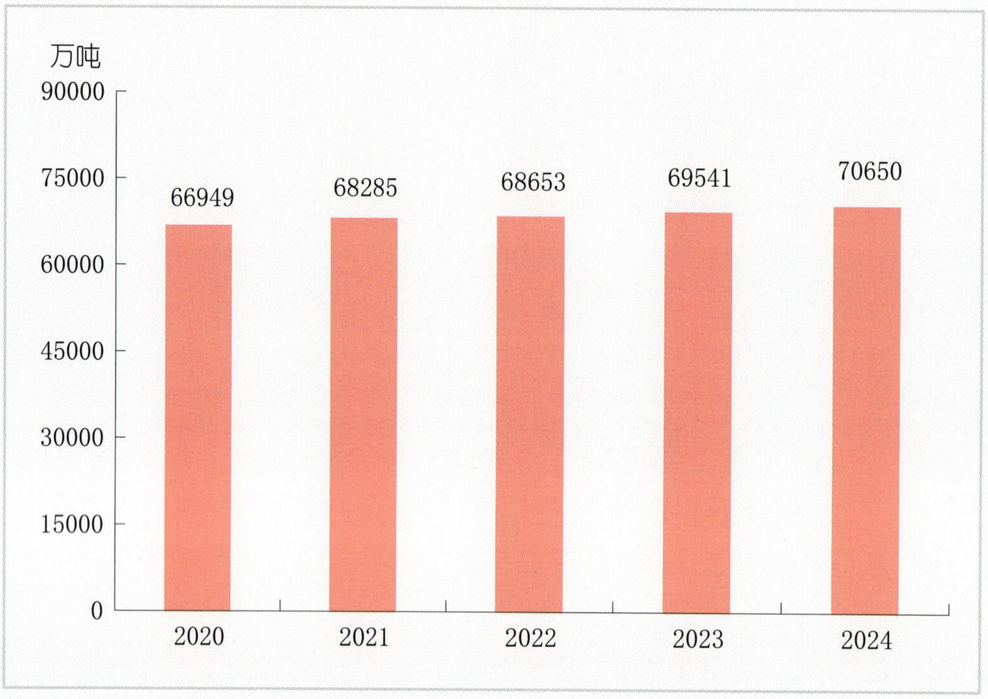

全年棉花产量616万吨，比上年增产9.7%。油料产量3979万吨，增产3.0%。糖料产量11870万吨，增产4.3%。茶叶产量374万吨，增产5.5%。

全年猪牛羊禽肉产量9663万吨，比上年增长0.2%。其中，猪肉产量5706万吨，下降1.5%；牛肉产量779万吨，增长3.5%；羊肉产量518万吨，下降2.5%；禽肉产量2660万吨，增长3.8%。禽蛋产量3588万吨，增长0.7%。牛奶产量4079万吨，下降2.8%。年末生猪存栏42743万头，比上年末下降1.6%；全年生猪出栏70256万头，比上年下降3.3%。

全年水产品总产量7366万吨，比上年增长3.5%。其中，养殖产量6062万吨，增长4.3%；捕捞产量1305万吨，下降0.1%。

全年木材产量13740万立方米，比上年增长8.2%。

三、工业和建筑业

全年全部工业增加值405442亿元，比上年增长5.7%。规模以上工业增加值增长5.8%。在规模以上工业中，分经济类型看，国有控股企业增加值增长4.2%；股份制企业增长6.1%，外商及港澳台投资企业增长4.0%；私营企业增长5.3%。分门类看，采矿业增长3.1%，制造业增长6.1%，电力、热力、燃气及水生产和供应业增长5.3%。

图 9　2020-2024 年全部工业增加值及其增长速度

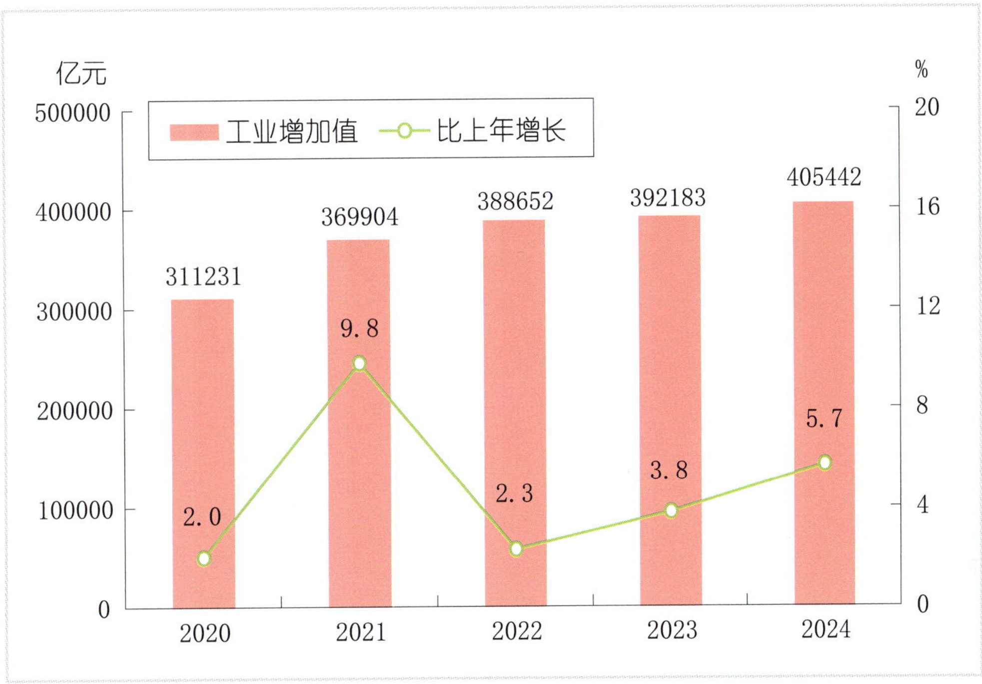

全年规模以上工业中，农副食品加工业增加值比上年增长2.2%，纺织业增长5.1%，化学原料和化学制品制造业增长8.9%，非金属矿物制品业下降1.4%，黑色金属冶炼和压延加工业增长4.0%，通用设备制造业增长3.6%，专用设备制造业增长2.8%，汽车制造业增长9.1%，电气机械和器材制造业增长5.1%，计算机、通信和其他电子设备制造业增长11.8%，电力、热力生产和供应业增长5.2%。

表3 2024年规模以上工业主要产品产量及其增长速度[22]

产品名称	单 位	产 量	比上年增长（%）
纱	万吨	2277.9	1.3
布	亿米	306.3	2.2
化学纤维	万吨	7910.8	9.7
成品糖	万吨	1498.6	17.0
卷烟	亿支	24654.6	0.9
彩色电视机	万台	20745.4	4.6
家用电冰箱	万台	10395.7	8.3
房间空气调节器	万台	26598.4	9.7
粗钢	万吨	100509.1	-1.7
钢材[23]	万吨	139967.4	1.1
十种有色金属	万吨	7918.8	4.3
其中：精炼铜（电解铜）	万吨	1364.4	4.1
原铝（电解铝）	万吨	4400.5	4.6
水泥	亿吨	18.3	-9.5
硫酸（折100%）	万吨	10369.9	6.9
烧碱（折100%）	万吨	4365.7	5.5
乙烯	万吨	3493.4	0.7
化肥（折100%）	万吨	6006.1	8.5
发电机组（发电设备）	万千瓦	28433.9	16.0
汽车	万辆	3155.9	4.8
其中：新能源汽车	万辆	1316.8	38.7
集成电路	亿块	4514.2	22.2
移动通信手持机	万台	166952.9	7.8
微型计算机设备	万台	33912.9	2.7
工业机器人	万套	55.6	14.2
太阳能工业用超白玻璃	万平方米	287884.5	53.5
充电桩	万个	469.7	58.7
智能手表	万个	8095.4	5.4
虚拟现实设备	万台	836.6	59.4

[22] 见注释[11]。
[23] 钢材产量数据中含企业之间重复加工钢材。

全年规模以上工业企业利润74311亿元，比上年下降3.3%。分经济类型看，国有控股企业利润21397亿元，比上年下降4.6%；股份制企业56166亿元，下降3.6%，外商及港澳台投资企业17638亿元，下降1.7%；私营企业23246亿元，增长0.5%。分门类看，采矿业利润11272亿元，比上年下降10.0%；制造业55141亿元，下降3.9%；电力、热力、燃气及水生产和供应业7898亿元，增长14.5%。规模以上工业企业每百元营业收入中的成本为85.16元，比上年增加0.36元；营业收入利润率为5.39%，下降0.30个百分点。年末规模以上工业企业资产负债率为57.5%，比上年末上升0.1个百分点。全年规模以上工业产能利用率[24]为75.0%。

初步核算，全年一次能源生产总量[25]49.8亿吨标准煤，比上年增长4.6%。

表4 2024年主要能源产品产量及其增长速度

产品名称	单 位	产 量	比上年增长（%）
原煤	亿吨	47.8	1.2
原油	万吨	21289.1	1.8
天然气	亿立方米	2464.5	6.0
发电量	亿千瓦时	100868.8	6.7
其中：火电[26]	亿千瓦时	63742.6	1.7
水电	亿千瓦时	14256.8	10.9
核电	亿千瓦时	4508.5	3.7
风电	亿千瓦时	9970.4	12.5
太阳能发电	亿千瓦时	8390.4	43.6

年末全国发电装机容量334862万千瓦，比上年末增长14.6%。其中[27]，火电装机容量144445万千瓦，增长3.8%；水电装机容量43595万千瓦，增长3.2%；核电装机容量6083万千瓦，增长6.9%；并网风电装机容量52068万千瓦，增长18.0%；并网太阳能发电装机容量88666万千瓦，增长45.2%。

全年建筑业增加值89949亿元，比上年增长3.8%。全国具有资质等级的总承包和专业承包建筑业企业利润7513亿元，比上年下降9.8%，其中国有控股企业利润3669亿元，下降8.7%。

[24] 产能利用率是指实际产出与生产能力（均以价值量计量）的比率。企业的实际产出是指企业报告期内的工业总产值；企业的生产能力是指报告期内，在劳动力、原材料、燃料、运输等保证供给的情况下，生产设备（机械）保持正常运行，企业可实现并能长期维持的产品产出。

[25] 根据《煤炭企业能源消费统计规范》（GB/T 28398—2023），煤炭洗选加工过程中产生的固体废弃物不计入煤炭消费量和综合能源消费量。据此对一次能源生产总量、能源消费总量、煤炭消费量统计核算口径进行了调整，2024年增速按可比口径计算。

[26] 火电包括燃煤发电量，燃油发电量，燃气发电量，余热、余压、余气发电量，垃圾焚烧发电量，生物质发电量。

[27] 少量发电装机容量（如地热等）公报中未列出。

图 10 2020-2024 年建筑业增加值及其增长速度

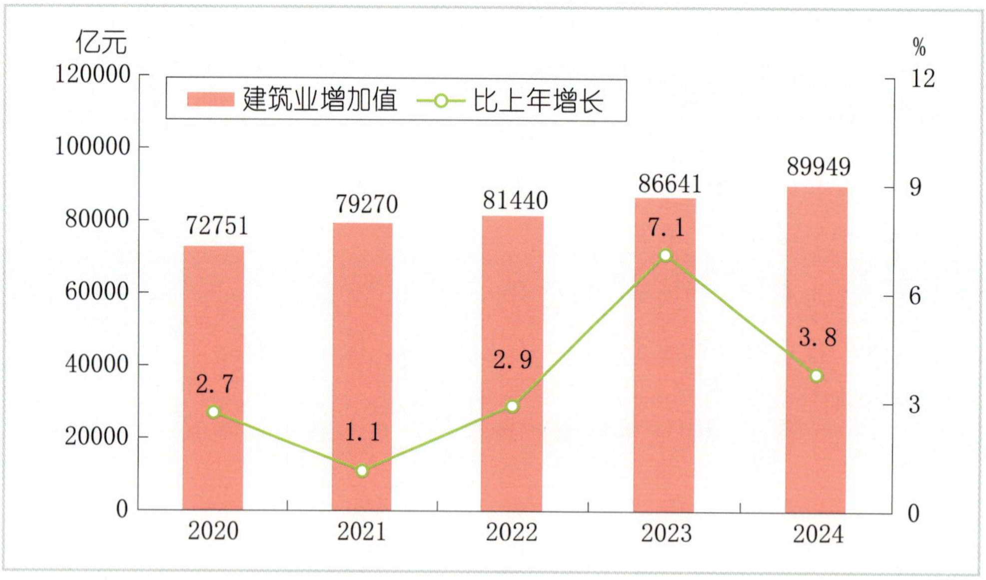

四、服务业

全年批发和零售业增加值137981亿元，比上年增长5.5%；交通运输、仓储和邮政业增加值59232亿元，增长7.0%；住宿和餐饮业增加值24729亿元，增长6.4%；金融业增加值98544亿元，增长5.6%；房地产业增加值84565亿元，下降1.8%；信息传输、软件和信息技术服务业增加值63438亿元，增长10.9%；租赁和商务服务业增加值56576亿元，增长10.4%。规模以上服务业企业营业收入比上年增长7.2%，利润总额增长2.4%。

图 11 2020-2024 年服务业增加值及其增长速度

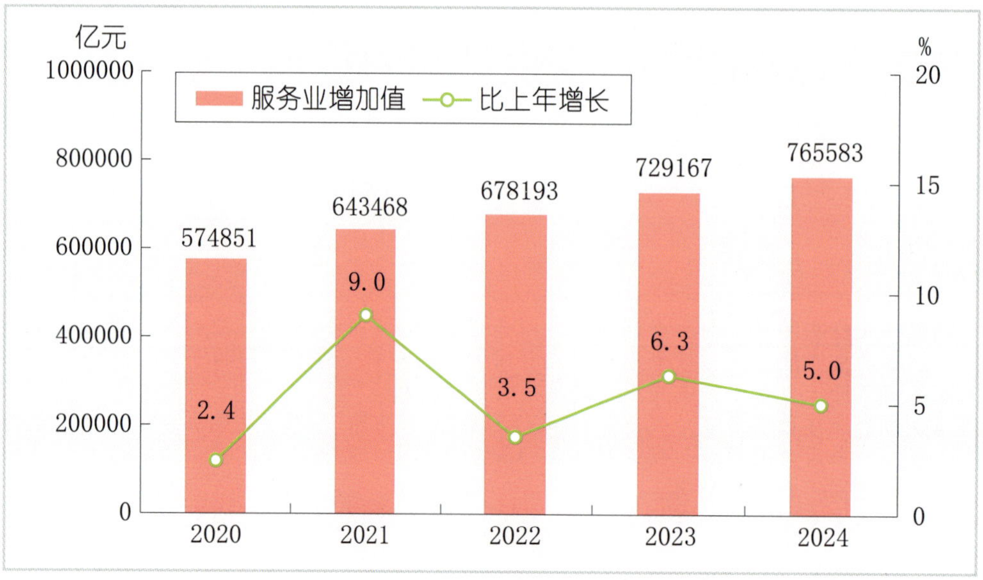

全年货物运输总量[28]578亿吨，比上年增长3.8%。货物运输周转量261948亿吨公里，增长5.6%。港口完成货物吞吐量176亿吨，比上年增长3.7%，其中外贸货物吞吐量54亿吨，增长6.9%。港口集装箱吞吐量33200万标准箱，增长7.0%。

表 5　2024 年各种运输方式完成货物运输量及其增长速度

指　标	单　位	绝对数	比上年增长（%）
货物运输总量	**亿吨**	**578.3**	**3.8**
铁路	亿吨	51.7	2.8
公路	亿吨	418.8	3.8
水路	亿吨	98.1	4.7
民航	万吨	898.2	22.1
管道	亿吨	9.5	-0.5
货物运输周转量	**亿吨公里**	**261948.1**	**5.6**
铁路	亿吨公里	35861.9	-1.6
公路	亿吨公里	76847.5	3.9
水路	亿吨公里	141422.9	8.8
民航	亿吨公里	353.9	24.8
管道	亿吨公里	7461.9	2.1

全年旅客运输总量[29]171亿人次，比上年增长8.5%。旅客运输周转量33886亿人公里，增长13.6%。

表 6　2024 年各种运输方式完成旅客运输量及其增长速度

指　标	单　位	绝对数	比上年增长（%）
旅客运输总量	**亿人次**	**170.8**	**8.5**
铁路	亿人次	43.1	11.9
公路	亿人次	117.8	7.0
水路	亿人次	2.6	0.8
民航	亿人次	7.3	17.9
旅客运输周转量	**亿人公里**	**33885.5**	**13.6**
铁路	亿人公里	15799.1	7.3
公路	亿人公里	5117.0	8.0
水路	亿人公里	54.7	1.7
民航	亿人公里	12914.7	25.3

[28] 货物运输总量及周转量包括铁路、公路、水路、民航和管道五种运输方式完成量，2024 年增速按可比口径计算。

[29] 自 2024 年 1 月起，公路旅客运输量、公路旅客运输周转量统计口径进行了调整，将班车包车客运量、公共汽电车城际城乡客运量、出租汽车（含巡游出租汽车、网络预约出租汽车）城际城乡客运量纳入公路旅客运输量统计，公路旅客运输周转量统计口径相应调整。2024 年旅客运输总量、旅客运输周转量、公路旅客运输量、公路旅客运输周转量增速按可比口径计算。

年末全国民用汽车保有量35268万辆（包括三轮汽车和低速货车694万辆），比上年末增加1651万辆，其中私人汽车保有量30989万辆，增加1562万辆；新能源汽车保有量3140万辆，增加1099万辆。民用轿车保有量19343万辆，增加675万辆，其中私人轿车保有量18204万辆，增加664万辆。

全年完成邮政行业寄递业务总量[30]1937亿件，比上年增长19.2%。邮政业完成邮政函件业务9.9亿件，包裹业务0.3亿件，快递业务量1751亿件，快递业务收入14034亿元。全年完成电信业务总量[31]18307亿元，比上年增长10.0%。年末移动电话基站数[32]1265万个，其中4G基站711万个，5G基站425万个。全国移动电话用户178960万户，其中5G移动电话用户101405万户。移动电话普及率为127.1部/百人。固定互联网宽带接入用户[33]66983万户，比上年末增加3352万户，其中1000M速率及以上的宽带接入用户[34]20683万户，增加4355万户。移动物联网终端用户[35]26.56亿户，增加3.24亿户。互联网上网人数11.08亿人，其中手机上网人数11.05亿人。互联网普及率为78.6%，其中农村地区互联网普及率为67.4%。全年移动互联网用户接入流量3376亿GB，比上年增长11.6%。软件和信息技术服务业[36]完成软件业务收入137276亿元，比上年增长10.0%。

图 12 2020-2024 年快递业务量及其增长速度[37]

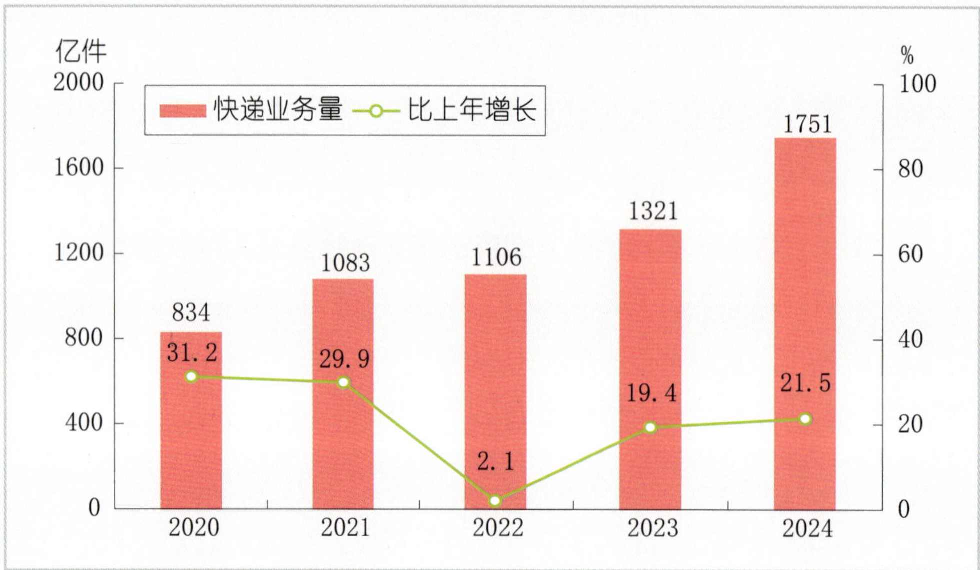

[30] 邮政行业寄递业务总量是指企业从事各类邮政普遍服务业务、快递业务的总数量。

[31] 电信业务总量按上年价格计算。

[32] 移动电话基站数是指报告期末为小区服务的无线收发信设备，处理基站与移动台之间的无线通信，在移动交换机与移动台之间起中继作用，监视无线传输质量的全套设备数。

[33] 固定互联网宽带接入用户是指报告期末在电信企业登记注册，通过 xDSL、FTTx+LAN、FTTH/O 以及其他宽带接入方式和普通专线接入公众互联网的用户。

[34] 1000M 速率及以上的宽带接入用户是指报告期末下行速率大于或等于 1000Mbit/s 的宽带接入用户。

[35] 移动物联网终端用户是指报告期末接入移动通信网络并开通物联网业务的用户。物联网终端即连接传感网络层和传输网络层，实现远程采集数据及向网络层发送数据的物联网设备。

[36] 软件和信息技术服务业包括软件开发、集成电路设计、信息系统集成和物联网技术服务、运行维护服务、信息处理和存储支持服务、信息技术咨询服务、数字内容服务和其他信息技术服务等行业。2024 年软件和信息技术服务业完成软件业务收入增速按可比口径计算。

[37] 2024 年快递业务量统计口径调整，增速按可比口径计算。

图 13　2020-2024 年年末固定互联网宽带接入用户数

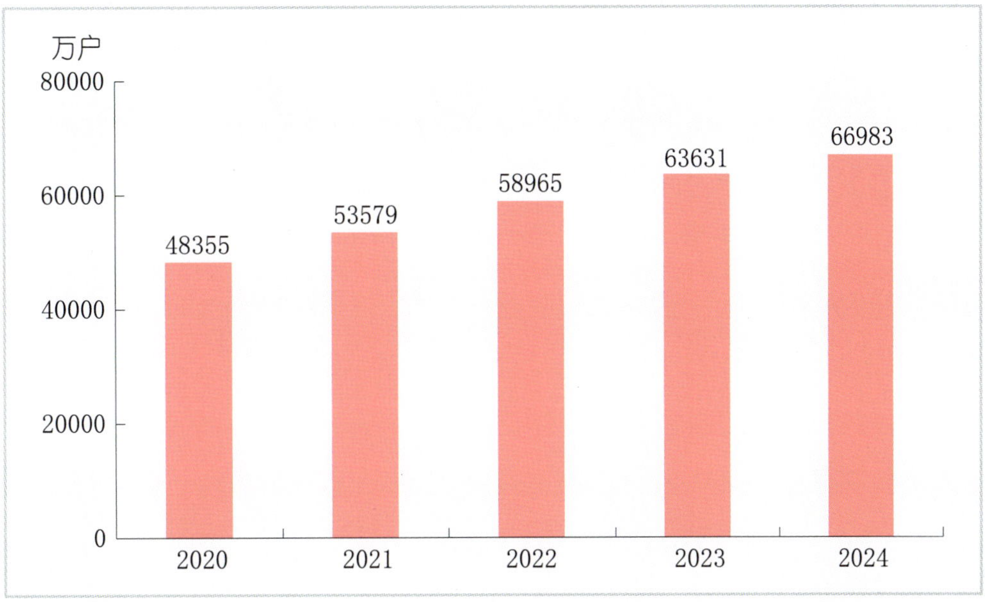

五、国内贸易

全年社会消费品零售总额[38]483345亿元，比上年增长3.5%。按经营地分，城镇消费品零售额417813亿元，增长3.4%；乡村消费品零售额65531亿元，增长4.3%。按消费类型分，商品零售额427165亿元，增长3.2%；餐饮收入56180亿元，增长5.3%。服务零售额[39]比上年增长6.2%。

图 14　2020-2024 年社会消费品零售总额及其增长速度

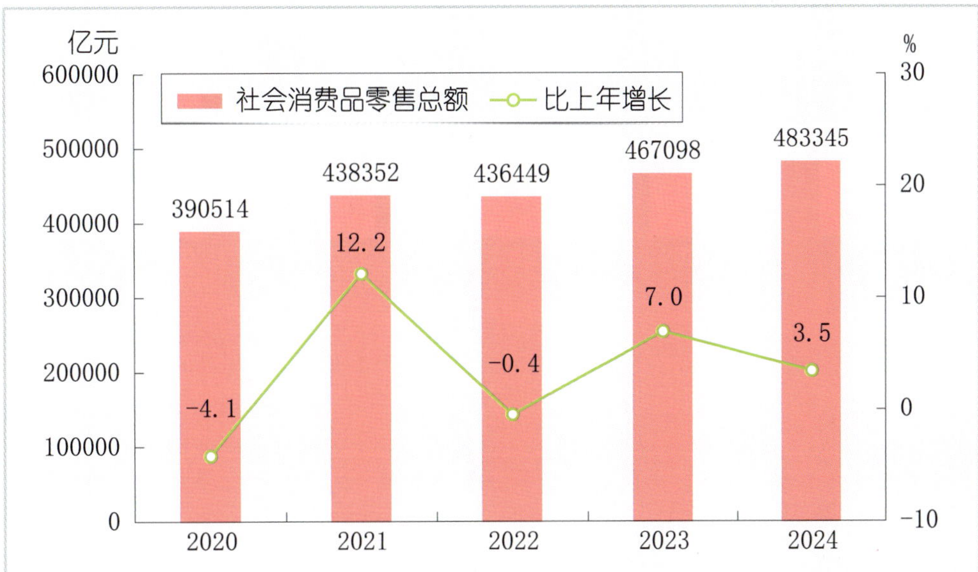

[38] 根据第五次全国经济普查结果对社会消费品零售总额数据进行修订。

[39] 服务零售额是指企业（产业活动单位、个体户）以交易形式直接提供给个人和其他单位非生产、非经营用的服务价值总和，旨在反映服务提供方以货币形式销售的属于消费的服务价值，包括交通、住宿、餐饮、教育、卫生、体育、娱乐等领域服务活动的零售额。

全年限额以上单位商品零售额中，粮油、食品类零售额比上年增长9.9%，饮料类增长2.1%，烟酒类增长5.7%，服装、鞋帽、针纺织品类增长0.3%，化妆品类下降1.1%，金银珠宝类下降3.1%，日用品类增长3.0%，体育、娱乐用品类增长11.1%，家用电器和音像器材类增长12.3%，中西药品类增长3.1%，文化办公用品类下降0.3%，家具类增长3.6%，通讯器材类增长9.9%，石油及制品类增长0.3%，汽车类下降0.5%，建筑及装潢材料类下降2.0%。按零售业态分，限额以上零售业单位中，便利店零售额比上年增长4.7%，专业店增长4.2%，超市增长2.7%，百货店下降2.4%，品牌专卖店下降0.4%。

全年实物商品网上零售额[40]127878亿元，比上年增长6.5%，占社会消费品零售总额比重为26.5%。

六、固定资产投资

全年全社会固定资产投资520916亿元，比上年增长[41]3.1%。固定资产投资（不含农户）514374亿元，增长3.2%，其中设备工器具购置投资增长15.7%。在固定资产投资（不含农户）中，分区域看[42]，东部地区投资增长1.3%，中部地区投资增长5.0%，西部地区投资增长2.4%，东北地区投资增长4.2%。

在固定资产投资（不含农户）中，第一产业投资9543亿元，比上年增长2.6%；第二产业投资179064亿元，增长12.0%；第三产业投资325767亿元，下降1.1%。基础设施投资[43]增长4.4%。社会领域投资[44]下降2.5%。民间投资[45]257574亿元，下降0.1%；扣除房地产开发民间投资，民间项目投资增长6.0%。分领域看，制造业民间投资增长10.8%，基础设施民间投资增长5.8%。

[40] 见注释[19]。

[41] 由于投资统计制度方法改革、第五次全国经济普查数据修订、统计执法检查等因素，2024年固定资产投资相关指标增速按可比口径计算。

[42] 见注释[20]。

[43] 基础设施投资包括铁路运输业、道路运输业、水上运输业、航空运输业、管道运输业、多式联运和运输代理业、装卸搬运业、邮政业、电信广播电视和卫星传输服务业、互联网和相关服务业、水利管理业、生态保护和环境治理业、公共设施管理业投资。

[44] 社会领域投资包括教育，卫生和社会工作，文化、体育和娱乐业投资。

[45] 民间投资是指具有集体、私营、个人性质的内资调查单位以及由其控股（包括绝对控股和相对控股）的调查单位在国内建造或购置固定资产的投资。

图15 2024年三次产业投资占固定资产投资（不含农户）比重

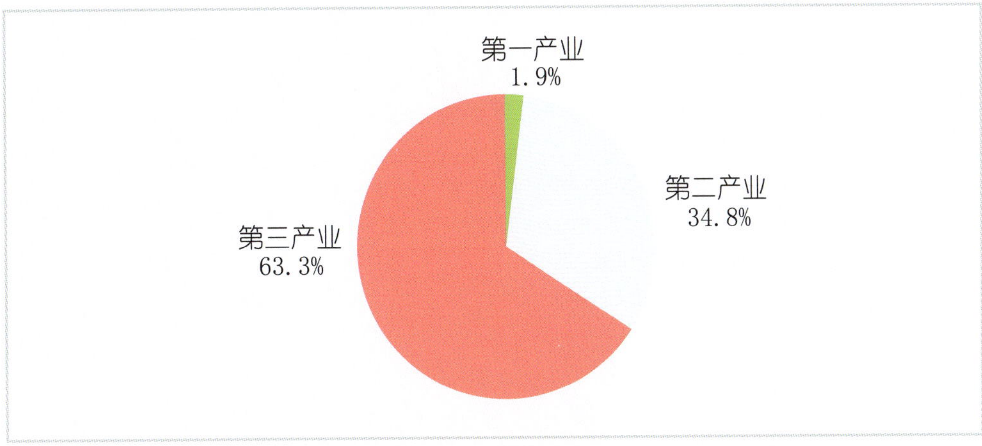

表7 2024年分行业固定资产投资（不含农户）增长速度

行　业	比上年增长（%）	行　业	比上年增长（%）
总　计	3.2	金融业	-6.3
农、林、牧、渔业	6.4	房地产业[46]	-10.8
采矿业	10.5	租赁和商务服务业	6.3
制造业	9.2	科学研究和技术服务业	11.8
电力、热力、燃气及水生产和供应业	23.9	水利、环境和公共设施管理业	4.2
建筑业	-1.9	居民服务、修理和其他服务业	0.7
批发和零售业	5.0	教育	1.3
交通运输、仓储和邮政业	5.9	卫生和社会工作	-9.4
住宿和餐饮业	34.1	文化、体育和娱乐业	0.0
信息传输、软件和信息技术服务业	6.3	公共管理、社会保障和社会组织	-4.2

表8 2024年固定资产投资新增主要生产与运营能力

指　标	单　位	绝对数
新增220千伏及以上交流变电设备容量	万千伏安	32119
新建铁路投产里程	公里	3113
其中：高速铁路	公里	2457
增、新建铁路复线投产里程	公里	2687
电气化铁路投产里程	公里	3936
新改建高速公路里程	公里	8968
港口万吨级及以上码头泊位新增通过能力	万吨/年	27106
新增民用运输机场	个	4
新增光缆线路长度	万公里	856

[46] 房地产业投资除房地产开发投资外，还包括建设单位自建房屋以及物业管理、中介服务和其他房地产投资。

全年房地产开发投资100280亿元，比上年下降[47]10.6%。其中住宅投资76040亿元，下降10.5%；办公楼投资4160亿元，下降9.0%；商业营业用房投资6944亿元，下降13.9%。全年新建商品房销售面积[48]97385万平方米。二手房交易网签面积[49]71812万平方米。年末新建商品房待售面积75327万平方米，其中商品住宅待售面积39088万平方米。

表 9 2024 年房地产开发和销售主要指标及其增长速度

指 标	单 位	绝对数	比上年增长（%）
房地产开发投资	亿元	100280	-10.6
其中：住宅	亿元	76040	-10.5
房屋施工面积	万平方米	733247	-12.7
其中：住宅	万平方米	513330	-13.1
房屋新开工面积	万平方米	73893	-23.0
其中：住宅	万平方米	53660	-23.0
房屋竣工面积	万平方米	73743	-27.7
其中：住宅	万平方米	53741	-27.4
新建商品房销售面积	万平方米	97385	-12.9
其中：住宅	万平方米	81450	-14.1
房地产开发企业本年到位资金	亿元	107661	-17.0
其中：国内贷款	亿元	15217	-6.1
个人按揭贷款	亿元	15661	-27.9

全年全国配售型保障性住房、保障性租赁住房和公租房等开工建设和筹集180万套（间）；城中村改造安置房开工建设和筹集189万套，城市危旧房改造开工7.9万套；新开工改造城镇老旧小区5.8万个，惠及居民966万户；农村低收入群体等重点对象农村危房改造和农房抗震改造开工23.9万户。

七、对外经济

全年货物进出口总额438468亿元，比上年增长5.0%。其中，出口254545亿元，增长7.1%；进口183923亿元，增长2.3%。货物进出口顺差70623亿元。对共建“一带一路”[50]国家进出口额220685亿元，比上年增长6.4%。其中，出口122095亿元，增长9.6%；进口98589亿元，增长2.7%。

[47] 根据第五次全国经济普查结果，对房地产开发、新建商品房销售等指标历史数据进行了修订，2024年增速按可比口径计算。

[48] 新建商品房销售面积是指报告期内房地产开发企业出售的新建商品房屋的合同总面积。

[49] 二手房交易网签面积是指报告期内城镇二手房网签交易合同总面积。

[50] “一带一路”是指“丝绸之路经济带”和“21 世纪海上丝绸之路”。

对《区域全面经济伙伴关系协定》（RCEP）其他成员国[51]进出口额131645亿元，比上年增长4.5%。民营企业进出口额243329亿元，比上年增长8.8%，占进出口总额比重为55.5%；其中出口164717亿元，增长9.4%。

图16 2020-2024年货物进出口总额

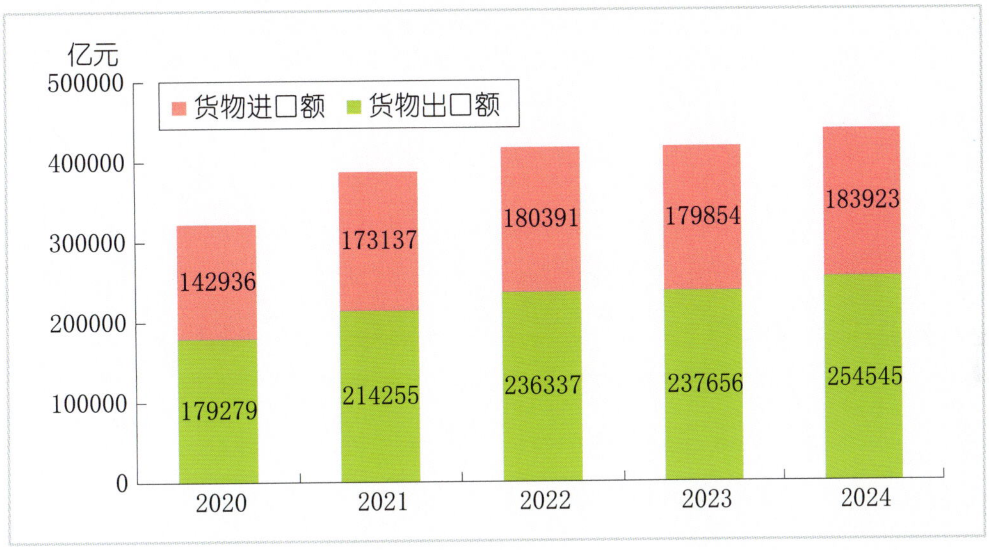

表10 2024年货物进出口总额及其增长速度

指　标	金额（亿元）	比上年增长（%）
货物进出口总额	**438468**	**5.0**
货物出口额	254545	7.1
其中：一般贸易	166466	8.5
加工贸易	50201	2.4
其中：机电产品	151246	8.7
高新技术产品	62792	6.0
货物进口额	183923	2.3
其中：一般贸易	114827	-1.9
加工贸易	28920	7.0
其中：机电产品	70095	7.3
高新技术产品	53584	11.9
货物进出口顺差	**70623**	**22.2**

[51]《区域全面经济伙伴关系协定》（RCEP）其他成员国包括印度尼西亚、马来西亚、菲律宾、泰国、新加坡、文莱、柬埔寨、老挝、缅甸、越南、日本、韩国、澳大利亚、新西兰。

表11 2024年主要商品出口数量、金额及其增长速度

商品名称	单 位	数 量	比上年增长（%）	金 额（亿元）	比上年增长（%）
钢材	万吨	11072	22.7	5950	0.4
纺织纱线、织物及其制品	—	—	—	10102	7.0
服装及衣着附件	—	—	—	11326	1.4
鞋靴	万双	920152	3.3	3336	-3.8
家具及其零件	—	—	—	4830	7.0
箱包及类似容器	万吨	362	9.6	2458	-2.0
玩具	—	—	—	2837	-0.7
塑料制品	—	—	—	7549	6.7
集成电路	亿个	2981	11.6	11352	18.7
自动数据处理设备及其零部件	—	—	—	14661	11.2
手机	万台	81394	1.5	9559	-2.4
集装箱	万个	545	135.7	1213	108.6
液晶平板显示模组	万个	189264	11.9	2066	10.3
汽车（包括底盘）	万辆	641	22.8	8347	16.5

表12 2024年主要商品进口数量、金额及其增长速度

商品名称	单 位	数 量	比上年增长（%）	金 额（亿元）	比上年增长（%）
大豆	万吨	10503	6.5	3751	-9.8
食用植物油	万吨	716	-26.8	528	-27.9
铁矿砂及其精矿	万吨	123655	4.9	9406	-1.4
煤及褐煤	万吨	54270	14.4	3705	-0.7
原油	万吨	55342	-1.9	23108	-2.7
成品油	万吨	4823	1.0	2083	5.7
天然气	万吨	13169	9.9	4637	2.5
初级形状的塑料	万吨	2898	-2.1	3117	-2.0
纸浆	万吨	3435	-6.3	1593	-4.3
钢材	万吨	681	-10.9	819	-8.1
未锻轧铜及铜材	万吨	568	3.4	3848	14.7
集成电路	亿个	5492	14.6	27445	11.7
汽车（包括底盘）	万辆	71	-11.7	2785	-16.1

表 13　2024 年对主要国家和地区货物进出口金额、增长速度及其比重

国家和地区	出口额（亿元）	比上年增长（%）	占全部出口比重（%）	进口额（亿元）	比上年增长（%）	占全部进口比重（%）
东盟	41736	13.4	16.4	28163	3.2	15.3
欧盟	36751	4.3	14.4	19164	-3.3	10.4
美国	37337	6.1	14.7	11641	1.2	6.3
韩国	10415	-0.5	4.1	12931	13.6	7.0
中国香港	20719	7.3	8.1	1321	37.8	0.7
日本	10816	-2.3	4.2	11119	-1.7	6.0
中国台湾	5350	11.0	2.1	15498	10.5	8.4
俄罗斯	8212	5.0	3.2	9198	1.0	5.0
巴西	5128	23.3	2.0	8258	-4.4	4.5
印度	8574	3.6	3.4	1280	-1.7	0.7
南非	1552	-6.5	0.6	2180	-3.0	1.2

全年服务进出口总额75238亿元，比上年增长14.4%。其中，出口31756亿元，增长18.2%；进口43482亿元，增长11.8%。服务进出口逆差11727亿元。

全年新设外商投资企业59080家，比上年增长9.9%。实际使用外资8263亿元，下降27.1%，折1162亿美元，下降28.8%。其中，共建“一带一路”国家（含通过部分自由港对华投资）对华新设外商投资企业17172家，增长23.8%；对华直接投资1147亿元，下降6.2%，折161亿美元，下降8.4%。高技术产业实际使用外资2864亿元，下降32.3%，折403亿美元，下降34.0%。

表 14　2024 年外商直接投资额及其增长速度

行　业	企业数（家）	比上年增长（%）	实际使用金额（亿元）	比上年增长（%）
总　计	59080	9.9	8263	-27.1
其中：农、林、牧、渔业	374	-10.5	27	-46.0
制造业	3871	6.8	2212	-30.4
电力、热力、燃气及水生产和供应业	439	-22.7	284	-10.9
交通运输、仓储和邮政业	838	-3.3	112	-25.0
信息传输、软件和信息技术服务业	3988	6.0	526	-53.6
批发和零售业	20854	15.8	584	-15.4
房地产业	612	-10.5	406	-49.9
租赁和商务服务业	11158	4.5	1815	-0.2
居民服务、修理和其他服务业	859	18.3	35	3.6

全年对外非金融类直接投资额10245亿元，比上年增长11.7%，折1438亿美元，增长10.5%。其中，对共建“一带一路”国家非金融类直接投资额2399亿元，增长6.5%，折337亿美元，增长5.4%。

表15 2024年对外非金融类直接投资额及其增长速度

行业	金额（亿美元）	比上年增长（%）
总计	1438	10.5
其中：农、林、牧、渔业	14	72.0
采矿业	125	80.1
制造业	296	6.2
电力、热力、燃气及水生产和供应业	64	109.5
建筑业	40	-40.0
批发和零售业	282	-3.6
交通运输、仓储和邮政业	74	13.7
信息传输、软件和信息技术服务业	58	18.8
房地产业	17	66.5
租赁和商务服务业	404	19.9

全年对外承包工程完成营业额11820亿元，比上年增长4.2%，折1660亿美元，增长3.1%。其中，对共建“一带一路”国家完成营业额1388亿美元，增长3.4%，占对外承包工程完成营业额比重为83.6%。对外劳务合作派出各类劳务人员41万人。

八、财政金融

全年全国一般公共预算收入219702亿元，比上年增长1.3%；其中税收收入174972亿元，下降3.4%。全国一般公共预算支出284612亿元，比上年增长3.6%。全年现行支持科技创新和制造业发展的主要政策减税降费及退税金额26293亿元。

图17 2020-2024年全国一般公共预算收入

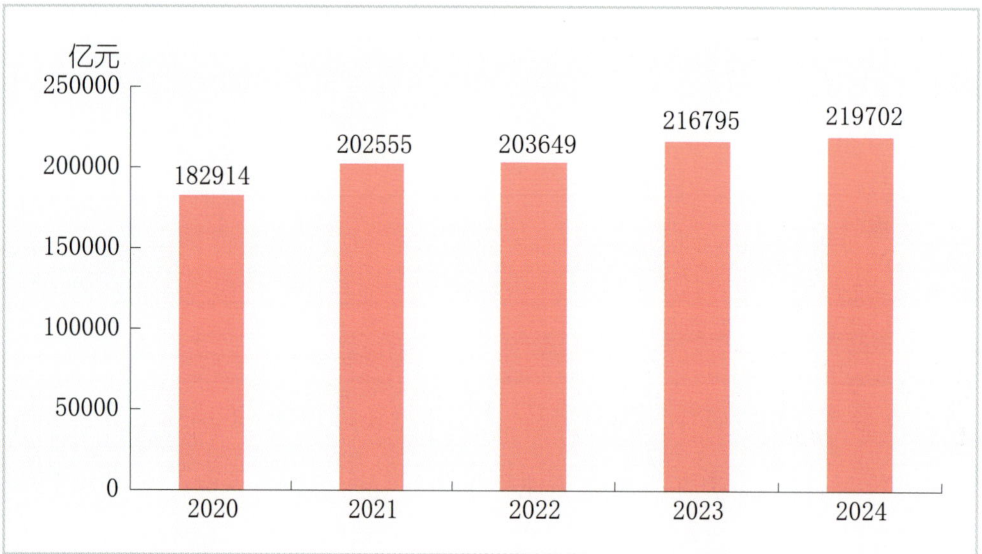

注：图中2020年至2023年数据为全国一般公共预算收入决算数，2024年为执行数。

年末广义货币供应量（M_2）余额313.5万亿元，比上年末增长7.3%；狭义货币供应量（M_1）余额67.1万亿元，下降1.4%；流通中货币（M_0）余额12.8万亿元，增长13.0%。

全年社会融资规模增量[52]32.3万亿元，按可比口径计算，比上年少3.3万亿元。年末社会融资规模存量[53]408.3万亿元，按可比口径计算，比上年末增长8.0%，其中对实体经济发放的人民币贷款余额252.5万亿元，增长7.2%。年末全部金融机构本外币各项存款余额308.4万亿元，比年初增加18.5万亿元，其中人民币各项存款余额302.3万亿元，增加18.0万亿元。全部金融机构本外币各项贷款余额259.6万亿元，增加17.3万亿元，其中人民币各项贷款余额255.7万亿元，增加18.1万亿元。人民币普惠小微贷款[54]余额32.9万亿元，增加4.2万亿元。本外币涉农贷款[55]余额51.4万亿元，增加4.7万亿元；制造业中长期贷款余额14.0万亿元，增加1.6万亿元；绿色贷款余额36.6万亿元，增加6.5万亿元。

表16　2024年年末全部金融机构本外币存贷款余额及其增长速度

指　标	年末数（亿元）	比上年末增长（%）
各项存款	**3083849**	6.4
其中：境内住户存款	1522529	10.4
其中：人民币	1512509	10.4
境内非金融企业存款	814791	-0.4
各项贷款	**2595750**	7.2
其中：境内短期贷款	653951	5.0
境内中长期贷款	1713857	7.7

年末主要农村金融机构（农村信用社、农村合作银行、农村商业银行）人民币贷款余额31.5万亿元，比年初增加2.1万亿元。全部金融机构人民币消费贷款余额58.7万亿元，增加0.7万亿元。其中，住户短期消费贷款余额10.2万亿元，减少0.2万亿元；住户中长期消费贷款余额48.5万亿元，增加0.9万亿元。

全年沪深交易所A股累计筹资[56]4251亿元，比上年减少6484亿元。沪深交易所首次公开发行上市A股77只，筹资622亿元，比上年减少2796亿元，其中科创板股票15只，筹资152亿元；沪深交

[52] 社会融资规模增量是指一定时期内实体经济从金融体系获得的资金总额。

[53] 社会融资规模存量是指一定时期末（月末、季末或年末）实体经济从金融体系获得的资金余额。

[54] 普惠小微贷款包括单户授信小于1000万元的小微企业贷款、个体工商户经营性贷款、小微企业主经营性贷款。

[55] 自2024年6月起，调整农村区域统计口径，将县城城区从农村区域中扣除。涉农贷款数据为可比口径数据。

[56] 沪深交易所股票筹资额按上市日统计，筹资额包括了可转债实际转股金额，2023年、2024年可转债实际转股金额分别为832亿元、1694亿元。

易所A股再融资（包括公开增发、定向增发、配股、优先股、可转债转股）3629亿元，减少3688亿元。北京证券交易所公开发行股票23只，筹资[57]48亿元。全年各类主体通过沪深北交易所发行债券（包括公司债券、企业债券、资产支持证券、国债和地方政府债券）筹资13.4万亿元，其中沪深交易所共上市基础设施领域不动产投资信托基金（REITs）29只，募集资金655亿元。全国中小企业股份转让系统挂牌公司6101家，全年挂牌公司累计股票筹资[58]119亿元。

全年发行公司信用类债券[59]14.8万亿元，比上年增加1.0万亿元。

全年保险公司原保险保费收入[60]56963亿元，按可比口径计算，比上年增长5.7%。其中，寿险业务原保险保费收入31917亿元，健康险和意外伤害险业务原保险保费收入10715亿元，财产险业务原保险保费收入14331亿元。支付各类赔款及给付23005亿元。其中，寿险业务给付8747亿元，健康险和意外伤害险业务赔款及给付4449亿元，财产险业务赔款9810亿元。

九、居民收入消费和社会保障

全年全国居民人均可支配收入41314元，比上年增长5.3%，扣除价格因素，实际增长5.1%。全国居民人均可支配收入中位数[61]34707元，增长5.1%。按常住地分，城镇居民人均可支配收入54188元，比上年增长4.6%，扣除价格因素，实际增长4.4%。城镇居民人均可支配收入中位数49302元，增长4.6%。农村居民人均可支配收入23119元，比上年增长6.6%，扣除价格因素，实际增长6.3%。农村居民人均可支配收入中位数19605元，增长4.6%。城乡居民人均可支配收入比值为2.34，比上年缩小0.05。按全国居民五等份收入分组[62]，低收入组人均可支配收入9542元，中间偏下收入组人均可支配收入21608元，中间收入组人均可支配收入33925元，中间偏上收入组人均可支配收入53359元，高收入组人均可支配收入98809元。全国农民工人均月收入4961元，比上年增长3.8%。脱贫县[63]农村居民人均可支配收入17522元，比上年增长6.9%，扣除价格因素，实际增长6.5%。

全年全国居民人均消费支出28227元，比上年增长5.3%，扣除价格因素，实际增长5.1%。其中，人均服务性消费支出[64]13016元，比上年增长7.4%，占居民人均消费支出比重为46.1%。按常住地分，城镇居民人均消费支出34557元，增长4.7%，扣除价格因素，实际增长4.5%；农村居民人

[57] 北京证券交易所股票筹资额按上市日统计。

[58] 全国中小企业股份转让系统挂牌公司累计筹资不含优先股，股票筹资按新增股份挂牌日统计。

[59] 公司信用类债券包括非金融企业债务融资工具、企业债券以及公司债、可转债等。

[60] 原保险保费收入是指保险企业确认的原保险合同保费收入。

[61] 人均可支配收入中位数是指将所有调查户按人均收入水平从低到高顺序排列，处于最中间位置调查户的人均可支配收入。

[62] 全国居民五等份收入分组是指将所有调查户按人均收入水平从低到高顺序排列，平均分为五个等份，处于最低20%的收入家庭为低收入组，依此类推依次为中间偏下收入组、中间收入组、中间偏上收入组、高收入组。

[63] 脱贫县包括原832个国家扶贫开发工作重点县和集中连片特困地区县，以及新疆阿克苏地区7个市县。

[64] 服务性消费支出是指住户用于各种生活服务的消费支出，包括餐饮服务、衣着鞋类加工服务、居住服务、家庭服务、交通通信服务、教育文化娱乐服务、医疗服务和其他服务。

均消费支出19280元，增长6.1%，扣除价格因素，实际增长5.8%。全国居民恩格尔系数为29.8%，其中城镇为28.8%，农村为32.3%。

图 18 2020-2024 年全国居民人均可支配收入及其增长速度

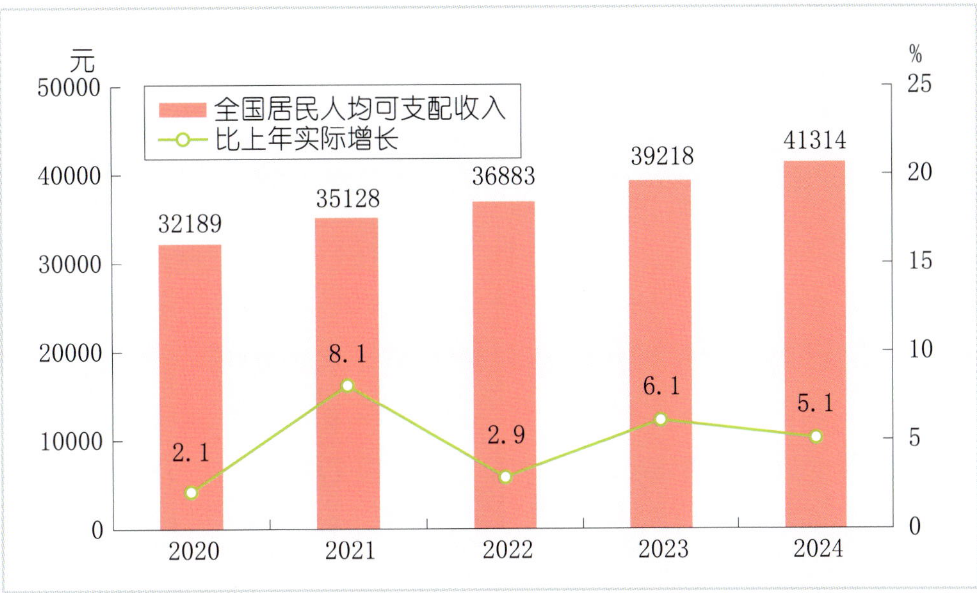

图 19 2024 年全国居民人均消费支出及其构成

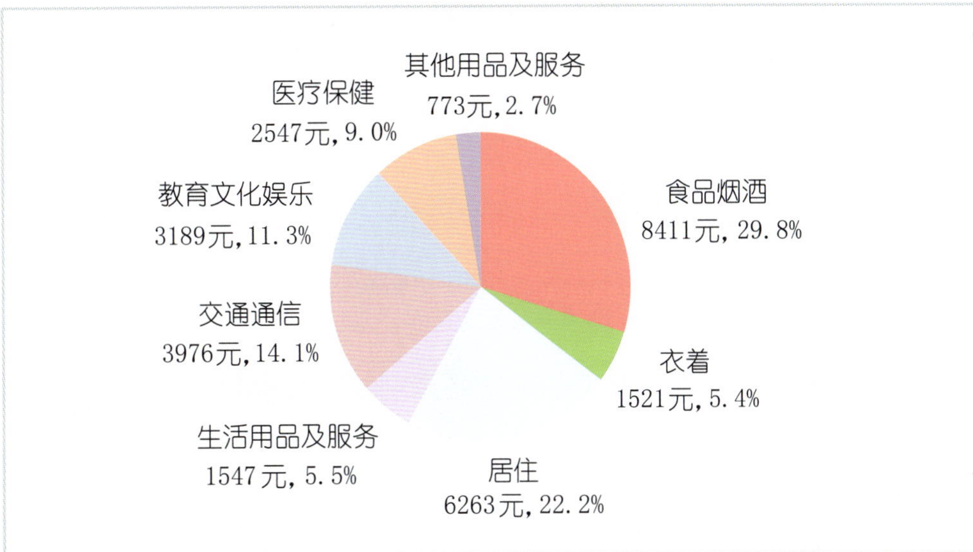

年末全国参加城镇职工基本养老保险人数53449万人，比上年末增加1329万人。参加城乡居民基本养老保险人数53830万人，减少692万人。参加基本医疗保险人数132638万人，其中参加职工基本医疗保险人数37920万人，参加城乡居民基本医疗保险人数94718万人。参加失业保险人数24589万人，增加216万人。参加工伤保险人数30398万人，增加224万人。参加生育保险人数25298万人。年末全国共有625万人享受城市最低生活保障，3362万人享受农村最低生活保障，439万人享受农村特困人员[65]救助供养，全年临时救助[66]772万人次。全年领取国家定期抚恤金、定期生活补助金的退役军人和其他优抚对象822万人。

年末全国共有各类提供住宿的民政服务机构4.3万个，其中养老机构4.0万个，儿童福利和救助保护机构1045个。民政服务床位[67]825.3万张，其中养老服务床位799.1万张，儿童福利和救助保护机构床位9.7万张。

十、科学技术和教育

全年研究与试验发展（R&D）经费支出36130亿元，比上年增长8.3%，与国内生产总值之比为2.68%，其中基础研究经费2497亿元，比上年增长10.5%，占R&D经费支出比重为6.91%。国家自然科学基金共资助5.49万个项目。截至年末，纳入新序列管理的国家工程研究中心206个，国家发展改革委认定的企业技术中心1798家。国家科技成果转化引导基金累计设立36只子基金，资金总规模624亿元。国家级科技企业孵化器[68]1606家，国家备案众创空间[69]2376家。全年授予发明专利权104.5万件，比上年增长13.5%。PCT专利申请受理量[70]7.5万件。截至年末，有效发明专利568.9万件，比上年末增长14.0%。每万人口高价值发明专利拥有量[71]14件。全年商标注册478.1万件，比上年增长9.1%。全年共签订技术合同99万项，技术合同成交金额68354亿元，比上年增长11.2%。我国公民具备科学素质[72]的比例达到15.37%。

[65] 农村特困人员是指无劳动能力，无生活来源，无法定赡养、抚养、扶养义务人或者其法定义务人无履行义务能力的农村老年人、残疾人以及未满16周岁的未成年人。

[66] 临时救助是指国家对遭遇突发事件、意外伤害、重大疾病或其他特殊原因导致基本生活陷入困境，其他社会救助制度暂时无法覆盖或救助之后基本生活暂时仍有严重困难的家庭或个人给予的应急性、过渡性的救助。

[67] 民政服务床位除收养性机构外，还包括救助类机构、社区类机构的床位。

[68] 国家级科技企业孵化器是指符合《科技企业孵化器管理办法》规定的，以促进科技成果转化、培育科技企业和企业家精神为宗旨，提供物理空间、共享设施和专业化服务的科技创业服务机构，且经过科学技术部批准确定的科技企业孵化器。

[69] 国家备案众创空间是指符合《发展众创空间工作指引》规定的新型创新创业服务平台，且按照《国家众创空间备案暂行规定》经科学技术部审核备案的众创空间。

[70] PCT专利申请受理量是指国家知识产权局作为PCT专利申请受理局受理的PCT专利申请数量。PCT(Patent Cooperation Treaty)即专利合作条约，是专利领域的一项国际合作条约。

[71] 每万人口高价值发明专利拥有量是指每万人口本国居民拥有的经国家知识产权局授权的符合下列任一条件的有效发明专利数量：战略性新兴产业的发明专利；在海外有同族专利权的发明专利；维持年限超过10年的发明专利；实现较高质押融资金额的发明专利；获得国家科学技术奖、中国专利奖的发明专利。

[72] 公民具备科学素质是指崇尚科学精神，树立科学思想，掌握基本科学方法，了解必要科技知识，并具有应用其分析判断事物和解决实际问题的能力。公民具备科学素质比例数据是面向18—69岁公民开展抽样调查获得。

图 20 2020-2024 年研究与试验发展（R&D）经费支出及其增长速度

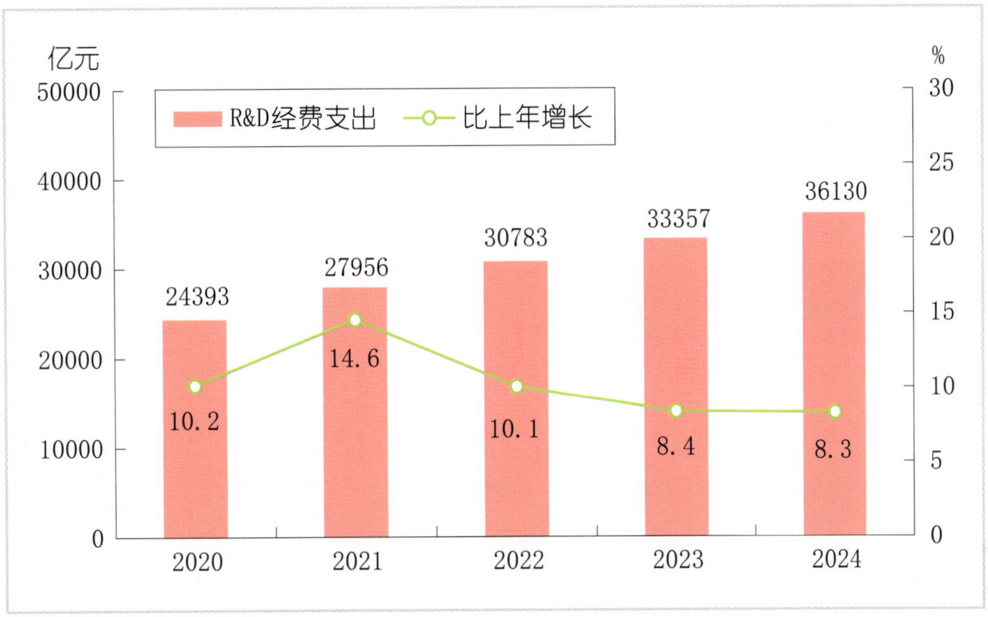

表 17 2024 年专利授权和有效专利情况

指　标	专利数（万件）	比上年增长（%）
发明专利授权	104.5	13.5
其中：境内发明专利授权	93.2	14.6
实用新型专利授权	201.0	-3.9
外观设计专利授权	64.3	0.8
年末有效发明专利	568.9	14.0
其中：境内有效发明专利	468.2	16.6
年末有效实用新型专利	1165.7	-3.9
年末有效外观设计专利	307.4	-4.9

全年完成68次宇航发射。“嫦娥六号”成功实现人类首次月球背面采样返回任务，首颗可重复使用返回式技术试验卫星实现成功回收，中国天眼FAST发现的脉冲星数量突破1000颗，全球首套高精度月球地质图集正式发布。中国环流三号（HL-3）等离子体电流突破1.5MA，首次成功构建超越经典计算机的量子模拟器，新一代气象超算系统建成。自主设计建造的首艘大洋钻探船“梦想”号交付入列，新一代中型隐身多用途战斗机在第15届珠海航展首次公开亮相。

年末全国共有国家质检中心874家。全国现有产品质量、体系和服务认证机构1230个，累计完成对110万家企业的认证。全年制定、修订国家标准3154项，其中新制定2001项。全年制造业产品质量合格率[73]为93.93%。

全年研究生教育招生135.7万人，在学研究生409.5万人，毕业生108.4万人。普通、职业本专科[74]招生1068.9万人，在校生3891.3万人，毕业生1059.4万人。中等职业教育[75]招生575.4万人，在校生1659.4万人，毕业生542.2万人。普通高中招生1036.2万人，在校生2922.3万人，毕业生891.0万人。初中招生1848.8万人，在校生5386.2万人，毕业生1698.2万人。普通小学招生1616.6万人，在校生10584.4万人，毕业生1857.3万人。特殊教育招生15.8万人，在校生91.6万人，毕业生17.7万人。学前教育在园幼儿3584.0万人。九年义务教育巩固率为95.9%，高中阶段毛入学率为92.0%。

图21　2020-2024年本专科、中等职业教育及普通高中招生人数

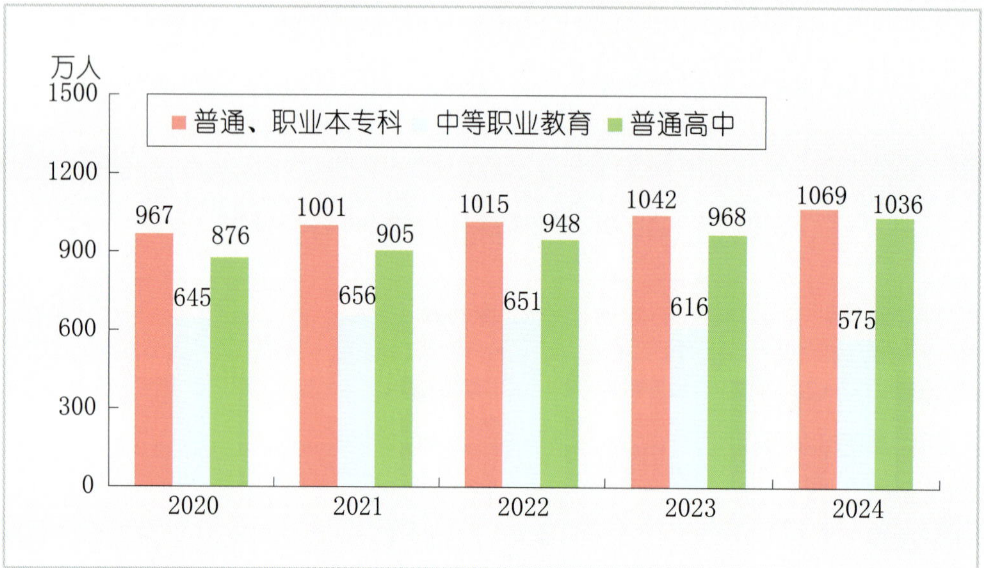

十一、文化旅游、卫生健康和体育

年末全国文化和旅游部门所属艺术表演团体1888个。全国共有公共图书馆3248个，总流通[76]134197万人次；文化馆3516个。有线电视实际用户2.09亿户，其中有线数字电视实际用户2.01亿户。年末广播节目综合人口覆盖率为99.7%，电视节目综合人口覆盖率为99.8%。全年生产电视剧115部3490集，电视动画片108271分钟。生产故事影片612部，科教、纪录、动画和特种影片[77]261部。出版

[73] 制造业产品质量合格率是指以产品质量检验为手段，按照规定的方法、程序和标准实施质量抽样检测，判定为质量合格的样品数占全部抽样样品数的百分比，统计调查样本覆盖制造业的29个行业。

[74] 普通、职业本专科包括普通本科、职业本科、高职（专科）。

[75] 中等职业教育包括普通中专、成人中专、职业高中和技工学校。

[76] 总流通人次是指本年度内到图书馆场馆接受图书馆服务的总人次，包括借阅书刊、咨询问题以及参加各类读者活动等。

[77] 特种影片是指采用与常规影院放映在技术、设备、节目方面不同的电影展示方式，如巨幕电影、立体特效（4D）电影、动感电影、球幕电影等。

各类报纸249亿份，各类期刊18亿册，图书118亿册（张），人均图书拥有量[78]8.39册（张）。年末全国共有档案馆4174个，已开放各类档案25238万卷（件）。全年全国规模以上文化及相关产业企业营业收入141510亿元，按可比口径计算，比上年增长6.0%。

全年国内出游56.2亿人次，比上年增长14.8%。其中，城镇居民国内出游43.7亿人次，增长16.3%；农村居民国内出游12.5亿人次，增长9.9%。国内游客出游总花费57543亿元，增长17.1%。其中，城镇居民出游花费49293亿元，增长18.0%；农村居民出游花费8250亿元，增长12.2%。入境游客13190万人次，增长60.8%，其中外国人2694万人次，香港、澳门和台湾同胞10496万人次。入境游客总花费942亿美元，增长77.8%。通过免签入境外国人2012万人次，增长112.3%。内地居民出境14589万人次，其中因私出境14015万人次，赴港澳台出境9712万人次。

图 22　2020-2024 年国内出游人次及其增长速度

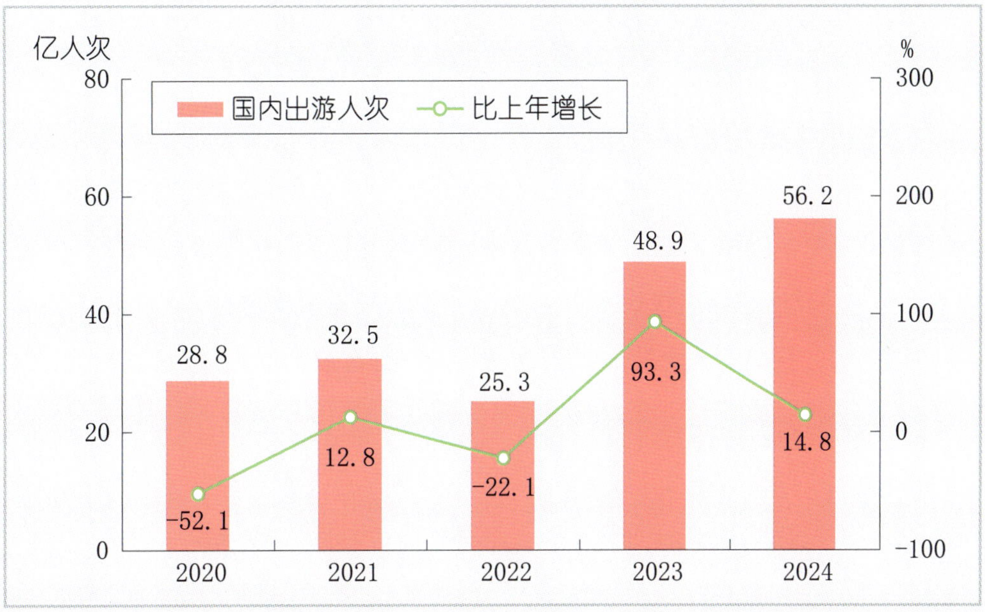

年末全国共有医疗卫生机构109.2万个，其中医院3.9万个，在医院中有公立医院1.2万个，民营医院2.7万个；基层医疗卫生机构104.0万个，其中乡镇卫生院3.3万个，社区卫生服务中心（站）3.7万个，门诊部（所）39.8万个，村卫生室57.1万个；专业公共卫生机构9217个（不含卫生监督所、中心），其中疾病预防控制中心3429个。卫生技术人员1295万人，其中执业医师和执业助理医师505万人，注册护士584万人。医疗卫生机构床位1037万张，其中医院818万张，乡镇卫生院151万张。全年总诊疗人次[79]101.1亿人次，出院人次[80]3.1亿人次。

---

[78] 人均图书拥有量是指在一年内全国平均每人能拥有的当年出版图书册数。

[79] 总诊疗人次是指所有诊疗工作的总人次数，包括门诊、急诊、出诊、预约诊疗、单项健康检查、健康咨询指导（不含健康讲座、核酸检测）人次数。

[80] 出院人次是指报告期内所有住院后出院的人次数，包括医嘱离院、医嘱转其他医疗机构、非医嘱离院、死亡及其他人次数，不含家庭病床撤床人次数。

图23 2020-2024年年末卫生技术人员人数

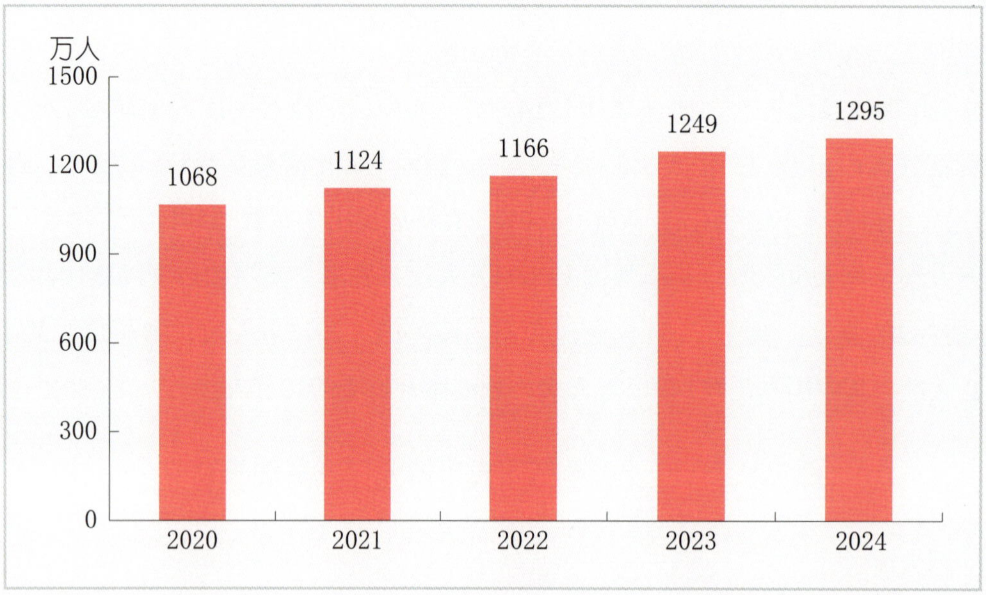

年末全国共有体育场地[81]484.2万个，体育场地面积[82]42.3亿平方米，人均体育场地面积3.0平方米。全年我国运动员在33个项目中获得194个世界冠军，共创19项世界纪录。在第33届奥运会上，我国运动员共获得40枚金牌，91枚奖牌，取得境外参加奥运会历史最好成绩，位列奥运会金牌榜并列第1位和奖牌榜第2位。我国残疾人运动员在45项国际赛事中获得333个世界冠军。在第17届残奥会上，我国运动员共获得94枚金牌，220枚奖牌，连续6次位列残奥会金牌榜和奖牌榜第1位。

十二、资源、环境和应急管理

全年全国国有建设用地供应总量[83]60.6万公顷，比上年下降19.1%。其中，工矿仓储用地15.5万公顷，下降11.5%；房地产用地[84]7.2万公顷，下降14.7%；基础设施用地38.0万公顷，下降22.5%。

全年水资源总量30010亿立方米。总用水量5925亿立方米，比上年增长0.3%。其中，生活用水增长1.9%，工业用水下降0.2%，农业用水下降0.7%，人工生态环境补水增长7.8%。万元国内生产总值用水量[85]46立方米，下降4.4%。万元工业增加值用水量25立方米，下降5.6%。人均用水量421立方米，增长0.4%。

[81] 体育场地调查对象不包括军队、铁路系统所属体育场地。
[82] 体育场地面积是指体育训练、比赛、健身场地的有效面积。
[83] 国有建设用地供应总量是指报告期内市、县人民政府根据年度土地供应计划依法以出让、划拨、租赁等方式与用地单位或个人签订出让合同或签发划拨决定书、完成交易的国有建设用地总量。
[84] 房地产用地是指商服用地和住宅用地的总和。
[85] 万元国内生产总值用水量、万元工业增加值用水量按2020年价格计算。

全年完成造林面积445万公顷，其中人工造林面积118万公顷，占全部造林面积的26.6%。种草改良面积[86]322万公顷。截至年末，共有国家公园5个。全年新增水土流失治理面积6.4万平方公里。

初步核算，全年能源消费总量[87]59.6亿吨标准煤，比上年增长4.3%。煤炭消费量增长1.7%，原油消费量下降1.2%，天然气消费量增长7.3%，电力消费量增长6.8%。煤炭消费量占能源消费总量比重为53.2%，比上年下降1.6个百分点；天然气、水电、核电、风电、太阳能发电等清洁能源消费量占能源消费总量比重为28.6%，上升2.2个百分点。重点耗能工业企业单位电石综合能耗下降0.8%，单位合成氨综合能耗下降1.2%，吨钢综合能耗下降0.1%，单位电解铝综合能耗下降0.2%，每千瓦时火力发电标准煤耗下降0.2%。初步测算，扣除原料用能和非化石能源消费量后，全国万元国内生产总值能耗[88]比上年下降3.8%。全国碳排放权交易市场碳排放配额[89]成交量1.89亿吨，成交额181.1亿元。

图 24　2020-2024 年清洁能源消费量占能源消费总量的比重

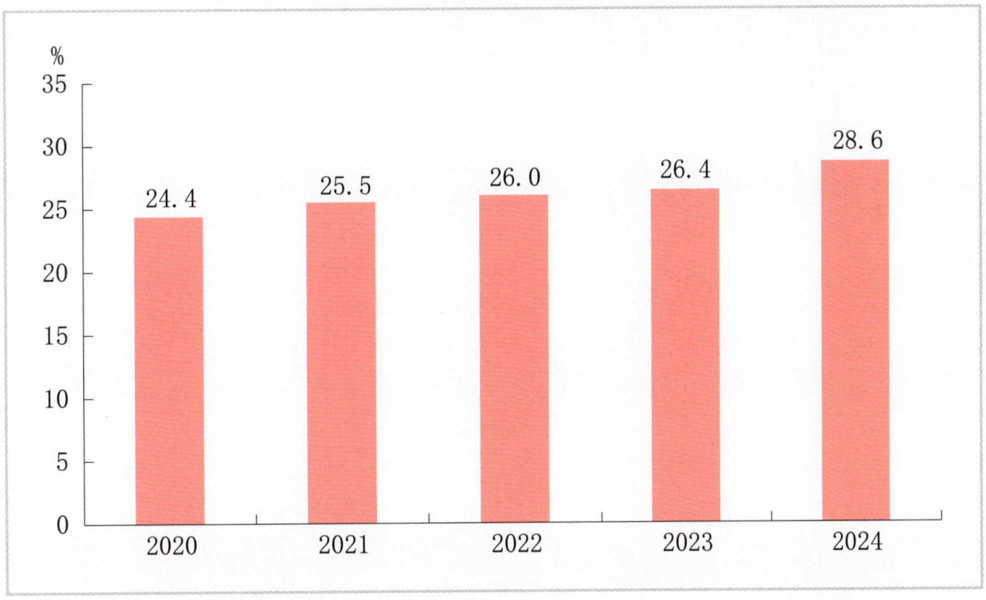

全年近岸海域海水水质[90]达到国家一、二类海水水质标准的面积占83.7%，三类海水占4.1%，四类、劣四类海水占12.2%。

[86] 种草改良面积是指通过人工种草、飞播种草、草原改良、围栏封育等措施进行草原生态修复的面积之和。

[87] 见注释 [25]。

[88] 万元国内生产总值能耗按 2020 年价格计算。

[89] 全国碳排放权交易市场碳排放配额是指在全国碳排放权交易市场分配给重点排放单位规定时期内的二氧化碳等温室气体的排放额度。1 个单位碳排放配额相当于向大气排放 1 吨的二氧化碳当量。

[90] 近岸海域海水水质采用面积法进行评价。

在监测的339个地级及以上城市中，细颗粒物（$PM_{2.5}$）年平均浓度29.3微克/立方米，比上年下降2.7%。

在开展城市区域声环境昼间监测的326个城市中，全年声环境质量好的城市占7.1%，较好的占66.9%，一般的占25.5%，较差的占0.6%，无差的城市。

全年平均气温为10.90℃，比上年上升0.19℃。共有9个台风登陆。

全年农作物受灾面积1009万公顷，其中绝收124万公顷。因洪涝和地质灾害造成直接经济损失2630亿元，因干旱灾害造成直接经济损失84亿元，因低温冷冻和雪灾造成直接经济损失256亿元，因海洋灾害造成直接经济损失109亿元。共发生5.0级以上地震25次，各级地震共造成直接经济损失38亿元。共发生森林火灾292起，受害森林面积约0.7万公顷。

全年各类生产安全事故共死亡19626人，比上年下降7.6%。工矿商贸企业就业人员10万人生产安全事故死亡人数1.089人，比上年下降12.5%；煤矿百万吨死亡人数0.059人，下降37.2%。道路交通事故万车死亡人数1.31人，下降5.1%。

资料来源：

本公报中城镇新增就业、养老保险、失业保险、工伤保险、中等职业教育中的技工学校数据来自人力资源和社会保障部；外汇储备、汇率数据来自国家外汇管理局；经营主体、质量检验、国家标准制定修订、制造业产品质量合格率数据来自国家市场监督管理总局；环境质量、碳排放权交易数据来自生态环境部；水产品产量数据来自农业农村部；木材产量、造林面积、种草改良面积、国家公园数据来自国家林业和草原局；发电装机容量、新增220千伏及以上交流变电设备容量、电力消费量数据来自中国电力企业联合会；港口货物吞吐量、港口集装箱吞吐量、公路运输、水路运输、新改建高速公路里程、港口万吨级及以上码头泊位新增通过能力数据来自交通运输部；铁路运输数据来自国家铁路局；民航运输、新增民用运输机场数据来自中国民用航空局；管道运输数据来自中国石油天然气集团有限公司、中国石油化工集团有限公司、中国海洋石油集团有限公司、国家石油天然气管网集团有限公司；民用汽车保有量、道路交通事故数据来自公安部；邮政业务数据来自国家邮政局；通信业、软件业务收入、国家级科技企业孵化器、国家备案众创空间、技术合同数据来自工业和信息化部；互联网上网人数、互联网普及率数据来自中国互联网络信息中心；新建铁路投产里程、增新建铁路复线投产里程、电气化铁路投产里程数据来自中国国家铁路集团有限公司；二手房交易网签面积、保障性住房、城中村改造、城市危旧房改造、城镇老旧小区改造、农村住房改造数据来自住房和城乡建设部；货物进出口数据来自海关总署；服务进出口、新设外商投资企业、实际使用外资、对外直接投资、对外承包工程、对外劳务合作数据来自商务部；财政数据来自财政部；减税降费及退税数据来自国家税务总局；货币金融、公司信用类债券数据来自中国人民银行；境内交易场所筹资数据来自中国证券监督管理委员会；保险业数据来自国家金融监督管理总局；医疗保险、生育保险数据来自国家医疗保障局；城乡低保、农村特困人员救助供养、临时救助、民政服务数据来自民政部；优抚对象数据来自退役军人事务部；国家自然科学基金资助项目数据来自国家自然科学基金委员会；国家工程研究中心、国家发展改革委认定的企业技术中心数据来自国家发展和改革委员会；国家科技成果转化引导基金数据来自科学技术部；专利、商标数据来自国家知识产权局；公民具备科学素质比例数据来自中国科学技术协会；宇航发射数据来自国家国防科技工业局；教育数据来自教育部；艺术表演团体、公共图书馆、文化馆、旅游数据来自文化和旅游部；电视、广播数据来自国家广播电视总局；电影数据来自国家电影局；报纸、期刊、图书数据来自国家新闻出版署；档案数据来自国家档案局；通过免签入境外国人、居民出境数据来自国家移民管理局；医疗卫生数据来自国家卫生健康委员会；体育数据来自国家体育总局；残疾人运动员数据来自中国残疾人联合会；国有建设用地供应、海洋灾害造成直接经济损失数据来自自然资源部；

水资源总量、用水量、新增水土流失治理面积数据来自水利部；平均气温、台风登陆数据来自中国气象局；农作物受灾面积、洪涝和地质灾害造成直接经济损失、干旱灾害造成直接经济损失、低温冷冻和雪灾造成直接经济损失、地震次数、各级地震造成直接经济损失、森林火灾、受害森林面积、生产安全事故数据来自应急管理部；其他数据均来自国家统计局。

STATISTICAL COMMUNIQUÉ OF THE PEOPLE'S REPUBLIC OF CHINA ON THE 2024 NATIONAL ECONOMIC AND SOCIAL DEVELOPMENT[1]

National Bureau of Statistics of China
February 28, 2025

The year 2024 marks the 75th anniversary of the founding of the People's Republic of China, and is a key year for achieving the goals and targets outlined in the 14th Five-Year Plan. Faced with complex and grave environment featuring greater external pressure and increasing internal difficulties, under the strong leadership of the Central Committee of the Communist Party of China (CPC) with Comrade Xi Jinping at its core, all regions and departments took Xi Jinping Thought on Socialism with Chinese Characteristics for a New Era as the guideline, fully implemented the guiding principles of the 20th CPC National Congress, the Second and the Third Plenary Sessions of the 20th CPC Central Committee, followed the decisions and arrangements made by the CPC Central Committee and the State Council, adhered to the general working guideline of making progress while maintaining stability, fully and faithfully applied the new development

1. All figures in this Communiqué are preliminary statistics. Statistics in this Communiqué do not include Hong Kong SAR, Macao SAR and Taiwan Province. Due to the rounding-off reasons, the subentries may not add up to the aggregate totals.

philosophy on all fronts, accelerated efforts to foster a new pattern of development, strove to promote high-quality development, comprehensively deepened reform and opening up, and strengthened macro control. As a result, the national economy was generally stable with steady progress made, high-quality development was pursued with solid steps, new quality productive forces witnessed steady development, reform and opening up continued to deepen, risks in key areas were defused with well-ordered and effective measures, people's wellbeing was strongly and effectively guaranteed, and new and solid strides were taken for Chinese modernization.

I. General Outlook

According to preliminary estimates, the gross domestic product (GDP)[2] in 2024 was 134,908.4 billion yuan, up by 5.0 percent over the previous year. Of this total, the value added of the primary industry was 9,141.4 billion yuan, up by 3.5 percent over the previous year, that of the secondary industry was 49,208.7 billion yuan, up by 5.3 percent, and that of the tertiary industry was 76,558.3 billion yuan, up by 5.0 percent. The value added of the primary industry accounted for 6.8 percent of the GDP; that of the secondary industry accounted for 36.5 percent; and that of the tertiary industry accounted for 56.7 percent. The contribution of the final consumption expenditure to GDP growth rate was up by 2.2 percentage points, that of the gross capital formation to GDP growth rate up by 1.3 percentage points and that of the net exports of goods and services to GDP growth rate up by 1.5 percentage points. By quarter, the GDP went up by 5.3 percent year on year for the first quarter, up by 4.7 percent for the second quarter, 4.6 percent for the third quarter and 5.4 percent for the fourth quarter. The per capita GDP in 2024 was 95,749 yuan, up by 5.1 percent over the previous year. The gross national income[3] in 2024 was 133,967.2 billion yuan, up by 5.1 percent over the previous year. The overall labor productivity[4] was 173,898 yuan per person, up by 4.9 percent over the previous year.

2. Gross domestic product (GDP), value added of the three and related industries, regional GDP, per capita GDP and gross national income (GNI) as quoted in this Communiqué are calculated at current prices whereas their growth rates are at constant prices. According to the results of the Fifth National Economic Census, and in light of the synchronous reform on the accounting methods of owner-occupied dwellings services for urban residents, historical data of GDP, value added of the three and related industries and overall labor productivity (including Figure 1, Figure 2, Figure 3, Figure 9, Figure 10 and Figure 11) were revised.

3. Gross national income, also known as gross national product, refers to the total primary distribution of the income created by all the resident units of a country (or a region) during a certain period of time. It equals to gross domestic product plus the net primary distribution of income from abroad.

4. The overall labor productivity refers to the ratio between the GDP (at 2020 constant prices) and the total number of persons employed.

Figure 1: Gross Domestic Product and Growth Rates 2020-2024

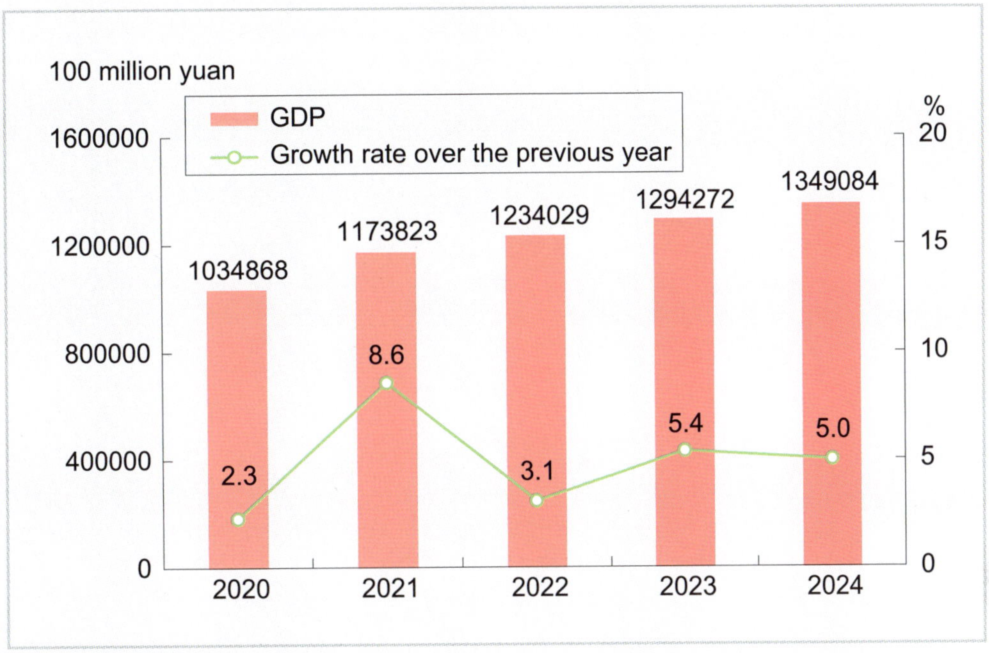

Figure 2: Shares of the Three Industries' Value Added in GDP 2020-2024

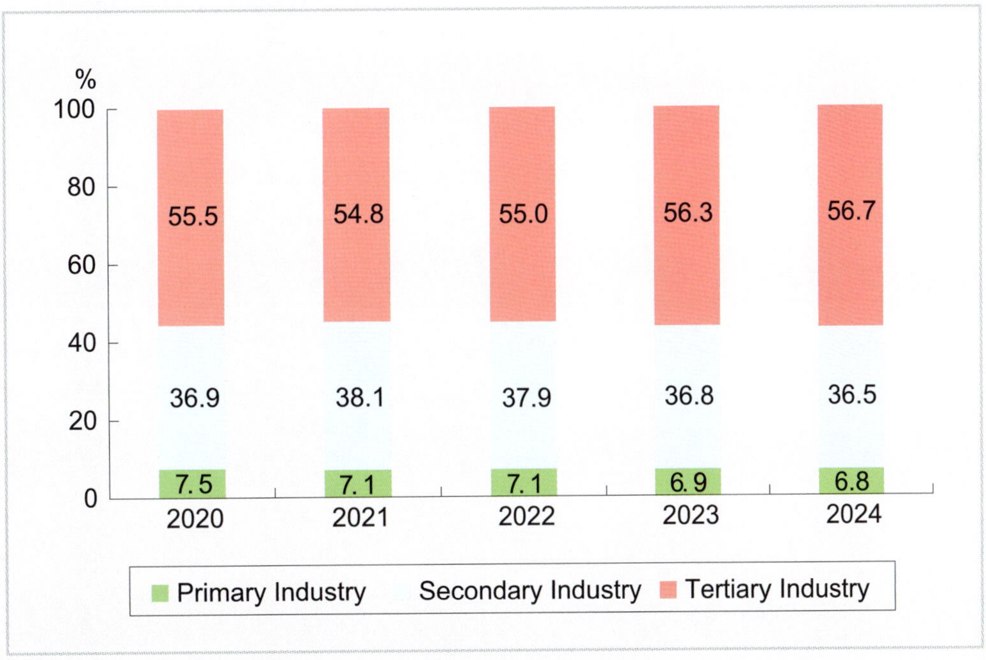

Figure 3: The Overall Labor Productivity 2020-2024

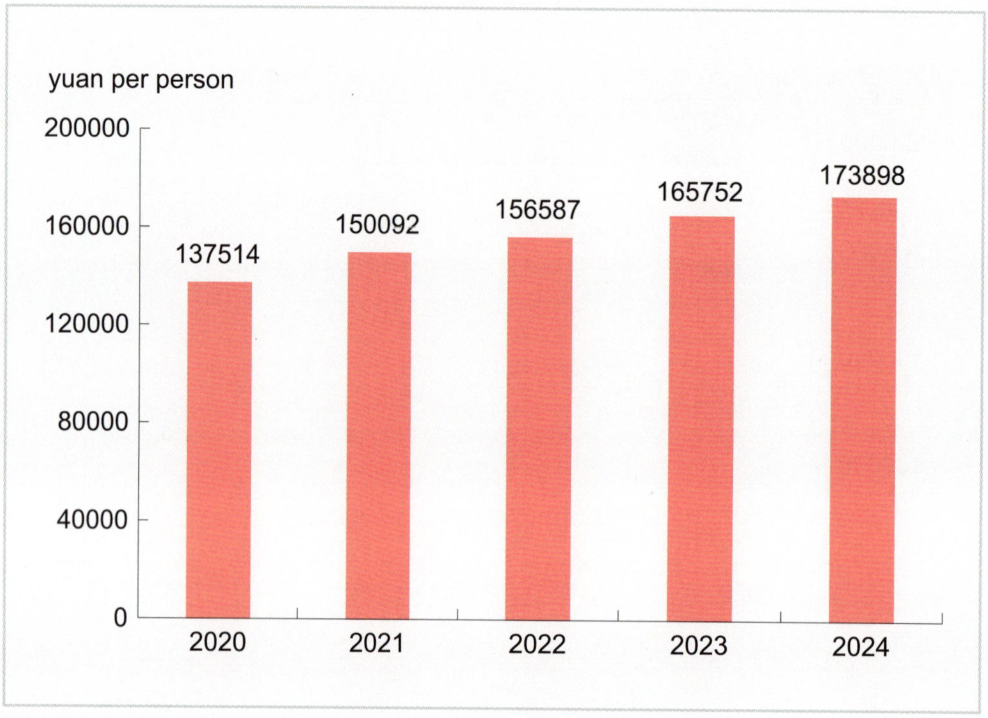

By the end of 2024, the total number of national population[5] reached 1,408.28 million, a decrease of 1.39 million over that at the end of 2023. Of this total, urban permanent residents numbered 943.50 million. There were 9.54 million births in 2024 with a crude birth rate of 6.77 per thousand; and there were 10.93 million deaths with a crude death rate of 7.76 per thousand. The natural growth rate was -0.99 per thousand.

Table 1: Population and Its Composition by the End of 2024

Item	Population at Year-end (10,000 persons)	Proportion (%)
National Total	**140828**	**100.0**
Of which: Urban	94350	67.0
Rural	46478	33.0
Of which: Male	71909	51.1
Female	68919	48.9
Of which: Aged 0-15 (under the age of 16)[6]	23999	17.1
Aged 16-59 (under the age of 60)	85798	60.9
Aged 60 and above	31031	22.0
Of which: Aged 65 and above	22023	15.6

5. The national population refers to the population of the 31 provinces, autonomous regions and municipalities directly under the central government and servicemen of the Chinese mainland, excluding residents of Hong Kong, Macao and Taiwan and foreigners living in the 31 provinces, autonomous regions and municipalities directly under the central government.

6. By the end of 2024, the population aged 0 to 14 (under the age of 15) was 222.40 million and that aged 15 to 59 (under the age of 60) was 875.57 million.

At the end of 2024, the number of employed people in China was 734.39 million, of which, that in urban areas was 473.45 million, accounting for 64.5 percent of the total employed people. The newly increased employed people in urban areas[7] numbered 12.56 million in 2024, 0.12 million more than that of the previous year. The urban surveyed unemployment rate in 2024 averaged 5.1 percent. The urban surveyed unemployment rate at the year end was 5.1 percent. The total number of migrant workers[8] was 299.73 million, up by 0.7 percent over that of 2023. Specifically, the number of migrant workers who left their hometowns and worked in other places was 178.71 million, up by 1.2 percent, and those who worked in their own localities reached 121.02 million, up by 0.1 percent.

Figure 4: Newly Increased Employed People in Urban Areas 2020-2024

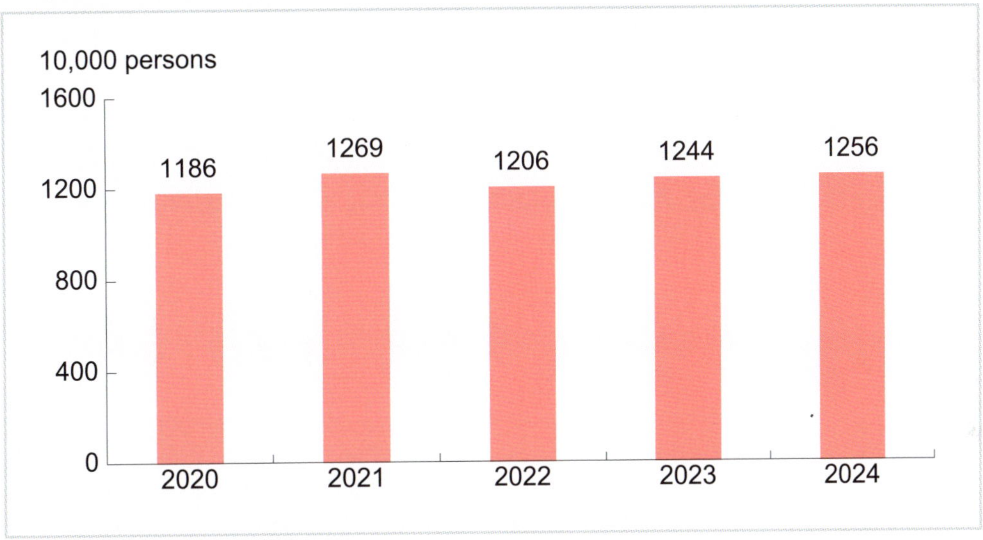

The consumer prices in 2024 went up by 0.2 percent over the previous year. The producer prices for industrial products went down by 2.2 percent and the purchasing prices for industrial producers down by 2.2 percent. The producer prices for farm products[9] dropped by 0.9 percent. In December, out of the 70 large and medium-sized cities, 23 cities experienced a month-on-month rise in sales prices of newly-built commercial residential buildings, 4 cities maintained the same level and 43 cities experienced a decline; 9 cities experienced a month-on-month rise in sales prices of second-hand housing, 1 city maintained the same

7. The number of newly increased employed people in urban areas equals the number of cumulative new employment minus the number of natural attrition in urban areas during the reporting period.

8. The number of migrant workers includes those who are employed outside their villages and towns for more than six months in the year and those who are engaged in non-agricultural work in their villages and towns for more than six months in the year.

9. The producer prices for farm products refer to the actual unit prices of farm products sold firsthand by producers.

level and 60 cities experienced a decline. Two cities experienced a year-on-year rise in sales prices of newly-built commercial residential buildings, and 68 cities experienced a decline. The number of cities experiencing a year-on-year decline in sales prices of second-hand housing was 70.

Figure 5: Monthly Changes of Consumer Prices in 2024

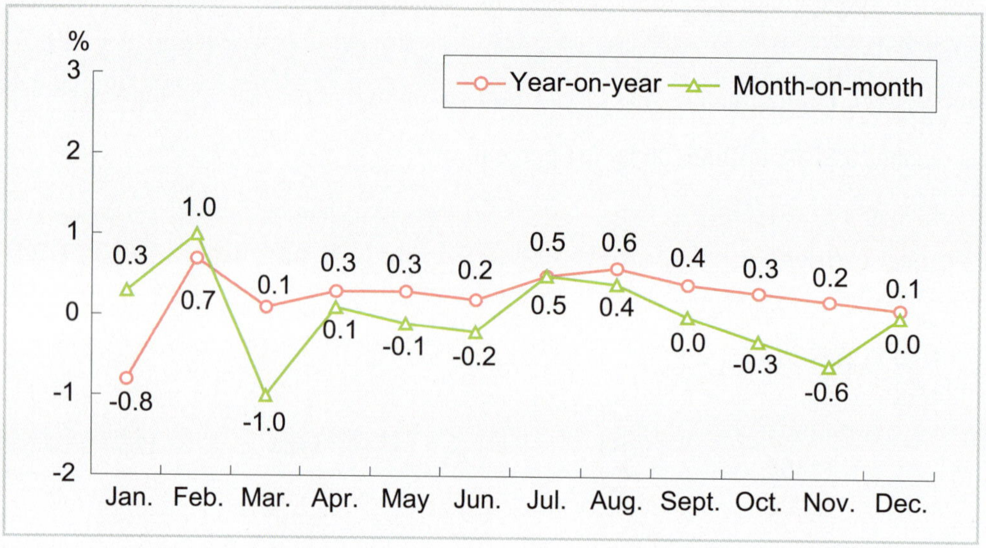

Table 2: Year-on-Year Changes of Consumer Prices in 2024

Unit: %

Item	National	Urban	Rural
General level of consumer prices	**0.2**	**0.2**	**0.3**
Of which: Food, tobacco and alcohol	-0.1	-0.1	-0.1
Clothing	1.4	1.6	0.9
Housing[10]	0.1	0.1	0.1
Articles and services for daily use	0.5	0.4	0.8
Transportation and communication	-1.9	-2.0	-1.5
Education, culture and recreation	1.5	1.5	1.6
Medical services and health care	1.3	1.2	1.5
Other articles and services	3.8	3.8	3.6

10. The prices for housing include prices for rent, maintenance and management, water, electricity and fuel, and services of owner-occupied dwellings etc.

At the end of 2024, China's foreign exchange reserves reached 3,202.4 billion US dollars, a decrease of 35.6 billion US dollars compared with that at the end of 2023. The average exchange rate of the year was 7.1217 RMB to 1 USD dollar, depreciated by 1.1 percent over that of 2023.

Figure 6: Year-end China's Foreign Exchange Reserves 2020-2024

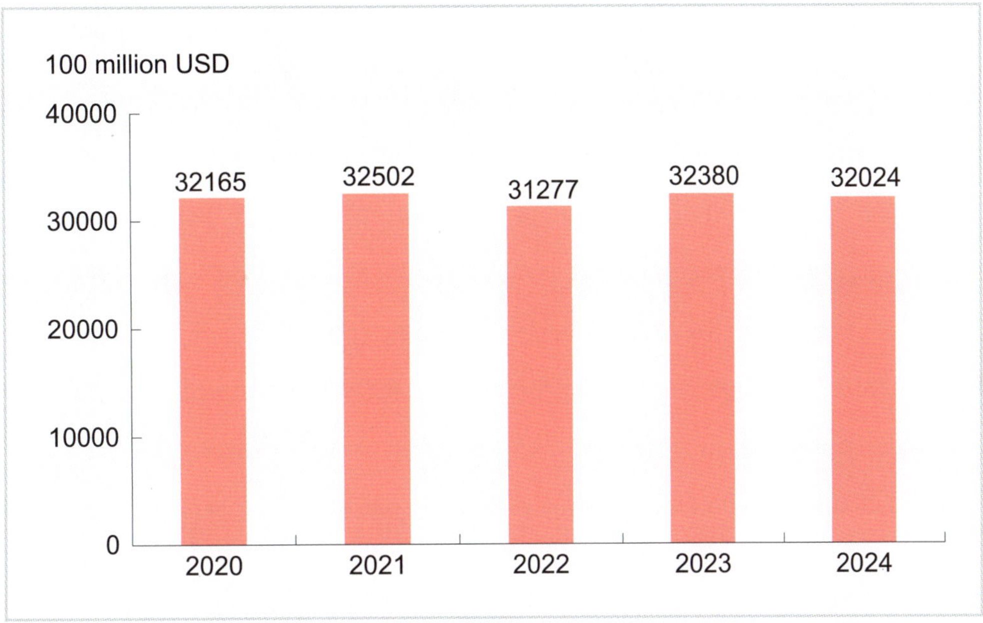

New quality productive forces developed at a steady pace. Among the industries above the designated size[11], the value added of the manufacture of equipment[12] was up by 7.7 percent over the previous year, accounting for 34.6 percent of that of all industrial enterprises above the designated size. The value added of the high technology manufacturing industry[13] increased by 8.9 percent, accounting for 16.3 percent of that of all industrial enterprises above the designated size. The output of new energy vehicles reached 13.168 million, up by 38.7 percent over the previous year; that of solar cells (photovoltaic cells) was 0.68 billion kilowatts, up by 15.7 percent; that of service robots reached 10.519 million, up by 15.6 percent; and that of 3D printing devices totaled 3.418 million, up by 11.3 percent. Among the service enterprises above the

11. The growth rates and rate changes of relevant indicators of the industries above the designated size in 2024 were calculated on a comparable basis due to adjustments of survey coverage in the statistical survey programs, statistical law enforcement and removal of duplicated data.

12. Manufacture of equipment includes manufacture of metal products, general purpose equipment, special purpose equipment, automobiles, railway, ship, aerospace and other transport equipment, electrical machinery and apparatus, computers, communication and other electric equipment and measuring instrument and machinery.

13. High technology manufacturing industry includes manufacture of medicine, manufacture of aerospace vehicle and equipment, manufacture of electronic and communication equipment, manufacture of computers and office equipment, manufacture of medical equipment, manufacture of measuring instrument and equipment and manufacture of optical and photographic equipment.

designated size[14], the business revenue of the strategic emerging service industries[15] went up by 7.9 percent compared with the previous year. The investment in high technology industries[16] increased by 8.0 percent over the previous year and the investment in technology transformation of manufacturing[17] grew by 8.0 percent. The e-commerce transactions[18] reached 46,409.1 billion yuan, up by 3.9 percent over the previous year. The online retail sales[19] reached 15,228.7 billion yuan, up by 7.2 percent over the previous year. In 2024, the number of newly established business entities was 27.37 million, with 24 thousand enterprises newly established per day on average.

Solid progress was made in the integrated development of urban and rural areas and coordinated regional development. By the end of 2024, the urbanization rate of permanent residents reached 67.00 percent, 0.84 percentage points higher than that at the end of 2023. By region[20], in 2024, the gross domestic product in the eastern region was 70,235.6 billion yuan, an increase of 5.0 percent over the previous year; the central region, 28,715.6 billion yuan, up by 5.0 percent; the western region, 28,735.0 billion yuan, up by 5.2 percent; and the northeastern region, 6,345.1 billion yuan, up by 4.4 percent. In 2024, the gross domestic product in Beijing-Tianjin-Hebei Region reached 11,539.4 billion yuan, up by 5.2 percent over the previous year; that in the Yangtze River Economic Belt, 63,022.8 billion yuan, up by 5.4 percent; and that

14. Service enterprises above the designated size refer to legal entities of transport, storage and post, information transmission, software and information technology services, water conservancy, environment and public facilities management, and health with annual business revenue of 20 million yuan and above; legal entities of real estate (excluding real estate development and operation), leasing and business services, scientific research and technical services and education with annual business revenue of 10 million yuan and above; and legal entities of household services, repair and other services, culture, sports and entertainment, and social services with annual business revenue of 5 million yuan and above. The growth rates of financial indicators of service enterprises above the designated size in 2024 were calculated on a comparable basis.

15. Strategic emerging service industries refer to the related service sectors of information technology of new generation, manufacture of high-end equipment, new materials, biotech, new energy vehicles, new energy, energy-saving and environmental protection and digital creative industries, and service industries related to new technology, innovation and entrepreneurship.

16. Investment in high technology industries refers to investment in six high technology manufacturing industries, including the manufacture of medicine and manufacture of aerospace vehicle and equipment, and nine high technology service industries, including information service and e-commerce service.

17. Investment in technology transformation of manufacturing refers to the investment by manufacturing enterprises in transformation of existing facilities, techniques and production services by adopting new technologies, techniques, devices and materials.

18. E-commerce transactions refer to the transactions of goods and services realized through e-commerce trading platforms (including self-built and third-party platforms), including transactions with entities and individuals. The historical data of e-commerce transactions were revised in accordance with the results of the Fifth National Economic Census. The growth rate of 2024 was calculated on a comparable basis.

19. Online retail sales refer to the retail sales of goods and services realized through internet trading platforms (online platforms mainly in trading physical goods, including self-built websites and third-party platforms). The data of online retail sales and online retail sales of physical goods were revised in accordance with the results of the Fifth National Economic Census. The growth rate of 2024 was calculated on a comparable basis.

20. The eastern region includes 10 provinces and municipalities: Beijing, Tianjin, Hebei, Shanghai, Jiangsu, Zhejiang, Fujian, Shandong, Guangdong and Hainan; the central region covers 6 provinces: Shanxi, Anhui, Jiangxi, Henan, Hubei and Hunan; the western region includes 12 provinces, autonomous regions and municipalities: Inner Mongolia, Guangxi, Chongqing, Sichuan, Guizhou, Yunnan, Xizang, Shaanxi, Gansu, Qinghai, Ningxia and Xinjiang; the northeastern region includes 3 provinces: Liaoning, Jilin and Heilongjiang.

in the Yangtze River Delta, 33,169.1 billion yuan, up by 5.5 percent. Major regional strategies such as the construction of Guangdong-Hong Kong-Macao Greater Bay Areas, and the ecological protection and high-quality development of the Yellow River Basin made new achievements.

Figure 7: Year-end Urbanization Rates of Permanent Residents 2020-2024

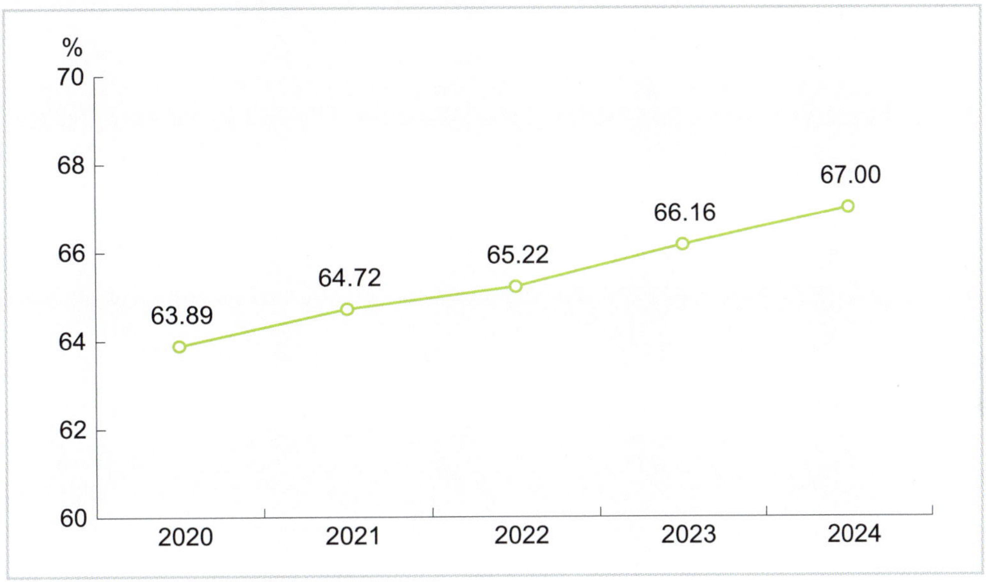

Green and low-carbon transformation was further promoted. According to preliminary estimates, the national carbon dioxide emissions per 10,000 yuan worth of GDP[21] in 2024 dropped by 3.4 percent over that of the previous year. The electricity generated by clean energy such as hydropower, nuclear power, wind power and solar power was 3,712.6 billion kilowatts-hours, up by 16.4 percent over the previous year. Of the monitored 339 cities at prefecture level and above, 65.5 percent reached the air quality standard and 34.5 percent failed. Of the 3,641 sections under the national monitoring program for surface water, 90.4 percent were of fairly clean water quality (Grade I to III), 7.8 percent were Grade IV, 1.2 percent were Grade V and 0.6 percent were worse than Grade V national standard.

II. Agriculture

In 2024, the sown area of grain was 119.32 million hectares, an increase of 0.35 million hectares compared with that in 2023. Of this total, the sown area of rice was 29.01 million hectares, an increase of 0.06 million hectares; the sown area of wheat was 23.59 million hectares, a decrease of 0.04 million hectares; the sown area of corn was 44.74 million hectares, an increase of 0.52 million hectares; the sown area of soybean

21. The carbon dioxide emissions per 10,000 yuan worth of GDP was calculated at 2020 constant prices.

was 10.33 million hectares, a decrease of 0.15 million hectares. The sown area of cotton was 2.84 million hectares, an increase of 0.05 million hectares. The sown area of oil-bearing crops was 14.29 million hectares, an increase of 0.37 million hectares; the sown area of sugar crops was 1.48 million hectares, an increase of 0.07 million hectares.

The total output of grain in 2024 was 706.50 million tons, an increase of 11.09 million tons over the previous year, up by 1.6 percent. Of this total, the output of summer crops was 149.89 million tons, up by 2.6 percent, that of the early rice was 28.17 million tons, down by 0.6 percent, and that of autumn grain was 528.43 million tons, up by 1.4 percent. The output of cereal was 652.29 million tons, up by 1.7 percent over that of 2023, among which the output of rice was 207.53 million tons, up by 0.5 percent; that of wheat was 140.10 million tons, up by 2.6 percent; and that of corn was 294.92 million tons, up by 2.1 percent. The output of soybean was 20.65 million tons, down by 0.9 percent over the previous year.

Figure 8: Output of Grain 2020-2024

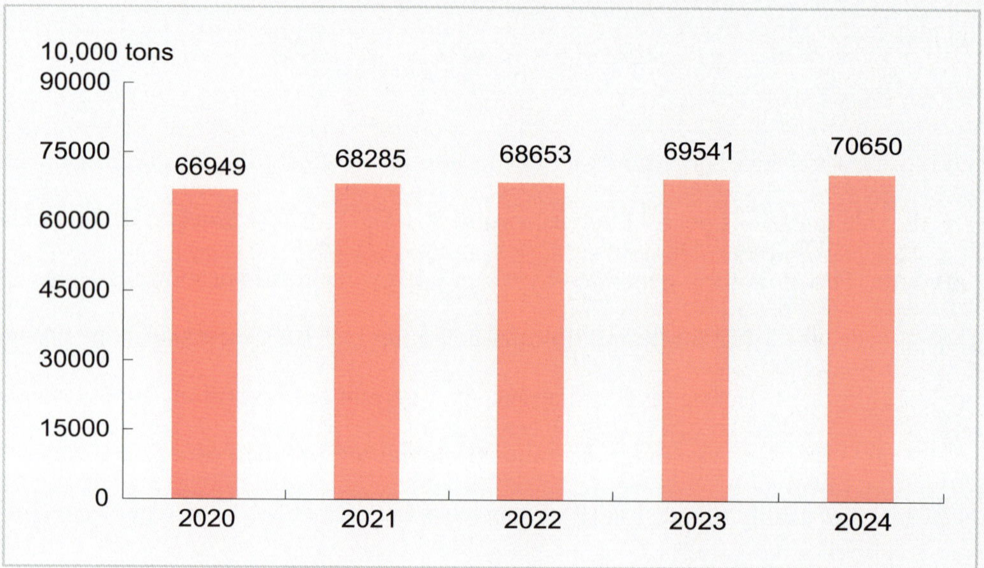

In 2024, the output of cotton was 6.16 million tons, up by 9.7 percent over the previous year, that of oil-bearing crops was 39.79 million tons, up by 3.0 percent, that of sugar crops was 118.70 million tons, up by 4.3 percent, and that of tea was 3.74 million tons, up by 5.5 percent.

The total output of pork, beef, mutton and poultry in 2024 was 96.63 million tons, up by 0.2 percent over the previous year. Of this total, the output of pork was 57.06 million tons, down by 1.5 percent; that of beef was 7.79 million tons, up by 3.5 percent; that of mutton was 5.18 million tons, down by 2.5 percent; and that of poultry was 26.60 million tons, up by 3.8 percent. The total output of eggs was 35.88

million tons, up by 0.7 percent. The output of milk was 40.79 million tons, down by 2.8 percent. At the end of the year, 427.43 million pigs were registered in the total stocks, down by 1.6 percent compared with that at the end of 2023, and 702.56 million pigs were slaughtered, down by 3.3 percent over the previous year.

The total output of aquatic products in 2024 was 73.66 million tons, up by 3.5 percent over the previous year. Of this total, the output of cultured aquatic products was 60.62 million tons, up by 4.3 percent; and that of fished aquatic products was 13.05 million tons, down by 0.1 percent.

The total production of timber in 2024 reached 137.40 million cubic meters, up by 8.2 percent over the previous year.

III. Industry and Construction

In 2024, the total value added of the industrial sector was 40,544.2 billion yuan, up by 5.7 percent over the previous year. The value added of industrial enterprises above the designated size increased by 5.8 percent. Of the industrial enterprises above the designated size, in terms of ownership, the value added of the state-holding enterprises was up by 4.2 percent, that of the share-holding enterprises up by 6.1 percent, that of the enterprises funded by foreign investors and investors from Hong Kong, Macao and Taiwan up by 4.0 percent and that of private enterprises up by 5.3 percent. In terms of sectors, the value added of the mining industry was up by 3.1 percent, that of manufacturing up by 6.1 percent and that of production and supply of electricity, heat power, gas and water up by 5.3 percent.

Figure 9: Value Added and Growth Rates of Industrial Enterprises 2020-2024

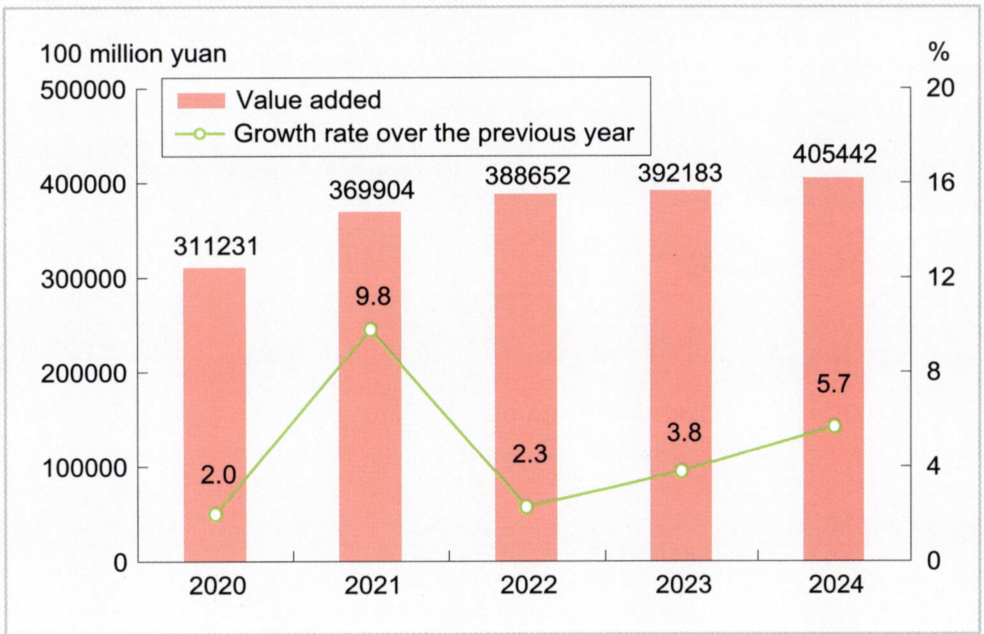

In 2024, of the industrial enterprises above the designated size, the value added for processing of food from agricultural and sideline products was up by 2.2 percent over the previous year; for textile industry up by 5.1 percent; for manufacture of raw chemical materials and chemical products up by 8.9 percent; for manufacture of non-metallic mineral products down by 1.4 percent; for smelting and pressing of ferrous metals up by 4.0 percent; for manufacture of general purpose machinery up by 3.6 percent; for manufacture of special purpose machinery up by 2.8 percent; for manufacture of automobiles up by 9.1 percent; for manufacture of electrical machinery and apparatus up by 5.1 percent; for manufacture of computers, communication equipment and other electronic equipment up by 11.8 percent; for production and supply of electricity and heat power up by 5.2 percent.

Table 3: Output of Major Industrial Products and Growth Rates of the Industrial Enterprises above the Designated Size in 2024[22]

Product	Unit	Output	Increase over 2023 (%)
Yarn	10000 tons	2277.9	1.3
Cloth	100 million meters	306.3	2.2
Chemical fiber	10000 tons	7910.8	9.7
Refined sugar (final product)	10000 tons	1498.6	17.0
Cigarettes	100 million	24654.6	0.9
Color TV sets	10000	20745.4	4.6
Household refrigerators	10000	10395.7	8.3
Air conditioners	10000	26598.4	9.7
Crude steel	10000 tons	100509.1	-1.7
Rolled steel[23]	10000 tons	139967.4	1.1
Ten kinds of nonferrous metals	10000 tons	7918.8	4.3
Of which: Refined copper (copper)	10000 tons	1364.4	4.1
Aluminum electrolyze	10000 tons	4400.5	4.6
Cement	100 million tons	18.3	-9.5
Sulfuric acid (100%)	10000 tons	10369.9	6.9
Caustic soda (100%)	10000 tons	4365.7	5.5
Ethylene	10000 tons	3493.4	0.7
Chemical fertilizer(100 percent equivalent)	10000 tons	6006.1	8.5
Power generation equipment	10000 kilowatts	28433.9	16.0
Motor vehicles	10000	3155.9	4.8
Of which: New energy vehicles	10000	1316.8	38.7
Integrated circuits	100 million pieces	4514.2	22.2
Mobile telephones	10000	166952.9	7.8
Micro computer equipment	10000	33912.9	2.7
Industrial robots	10000 sets	55.6	14.2
Ultra-clear glass for solar industry	10000 square meters	287884.5	53.5
Charging piles	10000	469.7	58.7
Smart watches	10000	8095.4	5.4
Virtual reality devices	10000	836.6	59.4

22. See Note 11.
23. The data included the steel reprocessed among enterprises.

In 2024, the profits made by industrial enterprises above the designated size were 7,431.1 billion yuan, down by 3.3 percent over the previous year. By ownership, the profits of state-holding enterprises were 2,139.7 billion yuan, down by 4.6 percent over the previous year; those of share-holding enterprises were 5,616.6 billion yuan, down by 3.6 percent; those of enterprises funded by foreign investors and investors from Hong Kong, Macao and Taiwan were 1,763.8 billion yuan, down by 1.7 percent; and those of private enterprises were 2,324.6 billion yuan, up by 0.5 percent. In terms of different sectors, the profits of mining were 1,127.2 billion yuan, down by 10.0 percent over the previous year; those of manufacturing were 5,514.1 billion yuan, down by 3.9 percent; and those of the production and supply of electricity, heat power, gas and water were 789.8 billion yuan, up by 14.5 percent. The cost for per-hundred-yuan business revenue of the industrial enterprises above the designated size was 85.16 yuan, 0.36 yuan more than that of 2023; the profit rate of the business revenue was 5.39 percent, 0.30 percentage points down. By the end of 2024, the asset-liability ratio of industrial enterprises above the designated size was 57.5 percent, 0.1 percentage points higher than that at the end of 2023. The capacity utilization rate[24] of industrial enterprises above the designated size was 75.0 percent in 2024.

According to preliminary estimates, the total primary energy output[25] in 2024 was 4.98 billion tons of standard coal equivalent, up by 4.6 percent over that of the previous year.

Table 4: Output of Major Energy Products and Growth Rates in 2024

Product	Unit	Output	Increase over 2023 (%)
Coal	100 million tons	47.8	1.2
Crude petroleum oil	10000 tons	21289.1	1.8
Natural gas	100 million cubic meters	2464.5	6.0
Electricity	100 million kilowatt-hours	100868.8	6.7
Of which:Thermal power[26]	100 million kilowatt-hours	63742.6	1.7
Hydropower	100 million kilowatt-hours	14256.8	10.9
Nuclear-power	100 million kilowatt-hours	4508.5	3.7
Wind power	100 million kilowatt-hours	9970.4	12.5
Solar power	100 million kilowatt-hours	8390.4	43.6

24. Capacity utilization rate refers to the ratio of the actual production to the production capacity (in terms of value). Actual production refers to the total industrial output value during the enterprise's reporting period. Production capacity refers to the production which can be realized and sustained for a long term under the condition of the supply of labor force, raw materials, fuel and transportation guaranteed and the production equipment in proper operation during the reporting period.

25. According to Statistical Rules on Energy Consumption of Coal Enterprises (GB/T 28398-2023), solid waste generated during coal washing and processing is not included in coal consumption and comprehensive energy consumption. On this basis, adjustments were made in statistical coverage of the total primary energy output, total energy consumption and coal consumption. The growth rates of 2024 were calculated on a comparable basis.

26. Thermal power refers to electricity generated by coal, oil, gas, residual heat, pressure and gas, waste incineration and biomass.

By the end of 2024, the installed power generation capacity was 3,348.62 million kilowatts, up by 14.6 percent over that at the end of 2023, among which[27] the installed thermal power generation capacity was 1,444.45 million kilowatts, up by 3.8 percent; the installed hydropower generation capacity was 435.95 million kilowatts, up by 3.2 percent; the installed nuclear power generation capacity was 60.83 million kilowatts, up by 6.9 percent; the installed grid-connected wind power generation capacity was 520.68 million kilowatts, up by 18.0 percent and the installed grid-connected solar power generation capacity was 886.66 million kilowatts, up by 45.2 percent.

In 2024, the value added of construction enterprises was 8,994.9 billion yuan, up by 3.8 percent over the previous year. The profits made by construction enterprises qualified for general contracts and specialized contracts reached 751.3 billion yuan, down by 9.8 percent over the previous year, of which the profits made by state-holding enterprises were 366.9 billion yuan, down by 8.7 percent.

Figure 10: Value Added and Growth Rates of Construction Industry 2020-2024

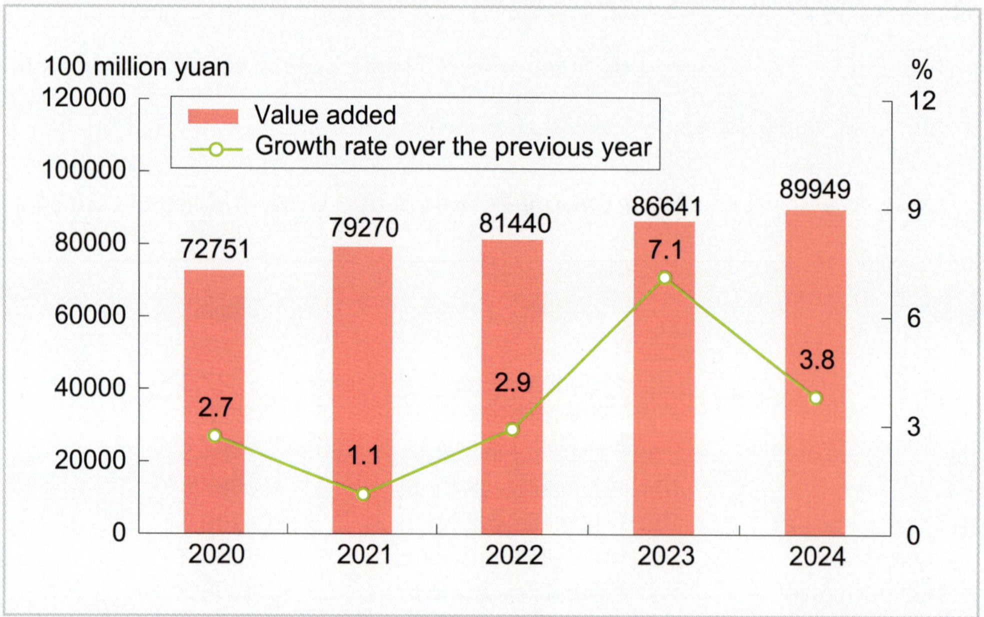

IV. Service Sector

In 2024, the value added of the wholesale and retail trades was 13,798.1 billion yuan, up by 5.5 percent over the previous year; that of transport, storage and post was 5,923.2 billion yuan, up by 7.0 percent; that of hotels and catering services was 2,472.9 billion yuan, up by 6.4 percent; that of finance was 9,854.4 billion

27. A few installed power generation capacity (e.g. geothermal) is not listed.

yuan, up by 5.6 percent; that of real estate was 8,456.5 billion yuan, down by 1.8 percent; that of information transmission, software and information technology services was 6,343.8 billion yuan, up by 10.9 percent; and that of leasing and business services was 5,657.6 billion yuan, up by 10.4 percent. The business revenue of service enterprises above the designated size grew by 7.2 percent over the previous year, and the total profits increased by 2.4 percent.

Figure 11: Value Added and Growth Rates of Service Sector 2020-2024

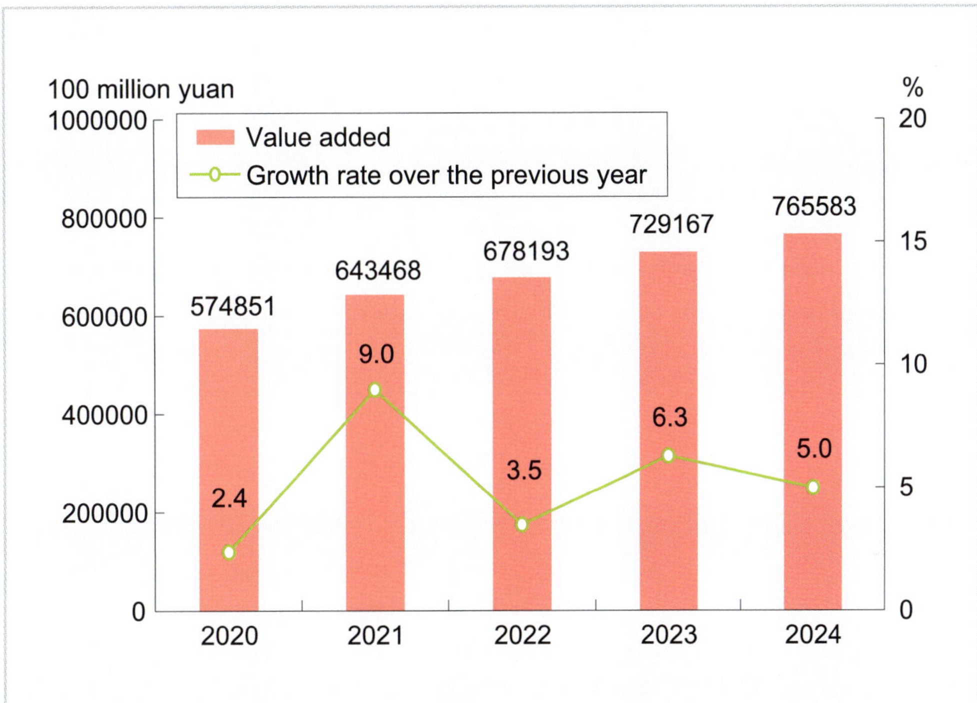

The total freight traffic[28] in 2024 reached 57.8 billion tons, up by 3.8 percent over the previous year. The freight flows were 26,194.8 billion ton-kilometers, up by 5.6 percent. The volume of freight handled by ports totaled 17.6 billion tons, up by 3.7 percent over the previous year, of which the freight for foreign trade was 5.4 billion tons, up by 6.9 percent. Container shipping of ports reached 332.00 million standard containers, up by 7.0 percent.

28. The total freight traffic and flows include the traffic and flows by railways, highways, waterways, civil aviation and pipelines. The growth rates in 2024 were calculated on a comparable basis.

Table 5: Freight Traffic by All Means of Transportation and Growth Rates in 2024

Item	Unit	Volume	Increase over 2023 (%)
Total freight traffic	**100 million tons**	**578.3**	**3.8**
Railways	100 million tons	51.7	2.8
Highways	100 million tons	418.8	3.8
Waterways	100 million tons	98.1	4.7
Civil aviation	10000 tons	898.2	22.1
Pipelines	100 million tons	9.5	-0.5
Freight flows	**100 million ton-kilometers**	**261948.1**	**5.6**
Railways	100 million ton-kilometers	35861.9	-1.6
Highways	100 million ton-kilometers	76847.5	3.9
Waterways	100 million ton-kilometers	141422.9	8.8
Civil aviation	100 million ton-kilometers	353.9	24.8
Pipelines	100 million ton-kilometers	7461.9	2.1

In 2024, the total passenger traffic[29] was 17.1 billion person-times, up by 8.5 percent over 2023, and the passenger flows were 3,388.6 billion person-kilometers, up by 13.6 percent.

Table 6: Passenger Traffic by All Means of Transportation and Growth Rates in 2024

Item	Unit	Volume	Increase over 2023 (%)
Total passenger traffic	**100 million person-times**	**170.8**	**8.5**
Railways	100 million person-times	43.1	11.9
Highways	100 million person-times	117.8	7.0
Waterways	100 million person-times	2.6	0.8
Civil aviation	100 million person-times	7.3	17.9
Passenger flows	**100 million person-kilometers**	**33885.5**	**13.6**
Railways	100 million person-kilometers	15799.1	7.3
Highways	100 million person-kilometers	5117.0	8.0
Waterways	100 million person-kilometers	54.7	1.7
Civil aviation	100 million person-kilometers	12914.7	25.3

The total number of motor vehicles for civilian use reached 352.68 million (including 6.94 million tri-wheel motor vehicles and low-speed trucks) by the end of 2024, up by 16.51 million over that at the end of

29. Since January 2024, the statistical coverage of highway passenger traffic and highway passenger flows has been adjusted with highway passenger traffic incorporating that of shuttle bus and chartered bus services, intercity and urban-rural bus services, and intercity and urban-rural taxi services (including cruising taxi and ride-hailing services), and highway passenger flows making corresponding adjustment. The growth rates of total passenger traffic, passenger flows, highway passenger traffic and highway passenger flows in 2024 were calculated on a comparable basis.

2023, of which the privately-owned vehicles numbered 309.89 million, an increase of 15.62 million; new energy vehicles totaled 31.40 million, up by 10.99 million. The total number of cars for civilian use was 193.43 million, an increase of 6.75 million, of which the privately-owned cars numbered 182.04 million, an increase of 6.64 million.

In 2024, the volume of postal and delivery services[30] totaled 193.7 billion, up by 19.2 percent over the previous year. The number of mail delivery was 0.99 billion; that of parcel delivery was 0.03 billion; and that of express delivery was 175.1 billion with a revenue reaching 1,403.4 billion yuan. The turnover of telecommunication services[31] in 2024 totaled 1,830.7 billion yuan, up by 10.0 percent over the previous year. By the end of 2024, there were 12.65 million mobile phone base stations[32], among which the number of 4G base stations reached 7.11 million and that of 5G base stations was 4.25 million. There were 1,789.60 million mobile phone subscribers in China, of whom 1,014.05 million were 5G mobile phone subscribers. The mobile phone coverage was 127.1 sets per 100 persons. The number of fixed broadband internet users[33] reached 669.83 million, an increase of 33.52 million over that at the end of the previous year. Of this total, users of broadband with the speed of 1000M and above[34] amounted to 206.83 million, an increase of 43.55 million. Users of mobile internet of things terminals[35] totaled 2.656 billion, an increase of 0.324 billion. The number of internet users was 1.108 billion, 1.105 billion of whom were mobile internet surfers. The coverage of internet was 78.6 percent, and 67.4 percent in rural areas. The mobile internet traffic in 2024 was 337.6 billion gigabytes, up by 11.6 percent over the previous year. Software revenue of software and information technology services industry[36] was 13,727.6 billion yuan, up by 10.0 percent over that of the previous year.

30. The volume of postal and delivery services refers to the total volume of universal postal services and express delivery services provided by enterprises.

31. The turnover of telecommunication services was calculated based on the prices of the previous year.

32. The number of mobile phone base stations refers to the total number of wireless transceivers serving communities that handle the wireless communication between the base stations and mobile stations, relay between the mobile switchboards and mobile stations, and monitor the quality of wireless transmission at the end of the reporting period.

33. Fixed broadband internet users refer to those who subscribe to the telecommunication enterprises and access the Internet through xDSL, FTTx+LAN, FTTH/O and other broadband access ways as well as general dedicated lines at the end of the reporting period.

34. Users of broadband with the speed of 1000M and above refer to those who enjoy a downstream rate of 1000Mbit/s or above at the end of the reporting period.

35. Users of mobile internet of things terminals refer to those who access the mobile internet and subscribe to the internet of things services at the end of the reporting period. Internet of things terminals refers to the internet of things devices that connect the sensing network layer and the transmission network layer to implement remote data collection and data transmission to the network layer.

36. Software and information technology services industry includes software development, integrated circuit design, information system integration and internet of things technology services, operation maintenance services, information processing and storage support services, IT consulting services, digital content services and other IT services industry. The growth rate of software revenue of software and information technology services industry in 2024 was calculated on a comparable basis.

Figure 12: Express Delivery and Growth Rates 2020-2024[37]

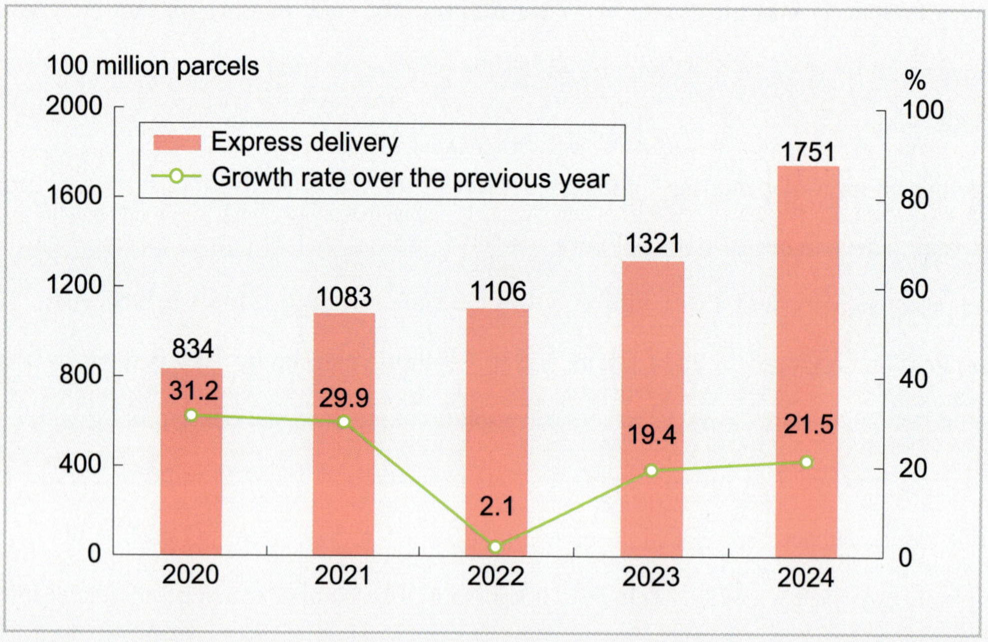

Figure 13: Year-end Number of Fixed Broadband Internet Users 2020-2024

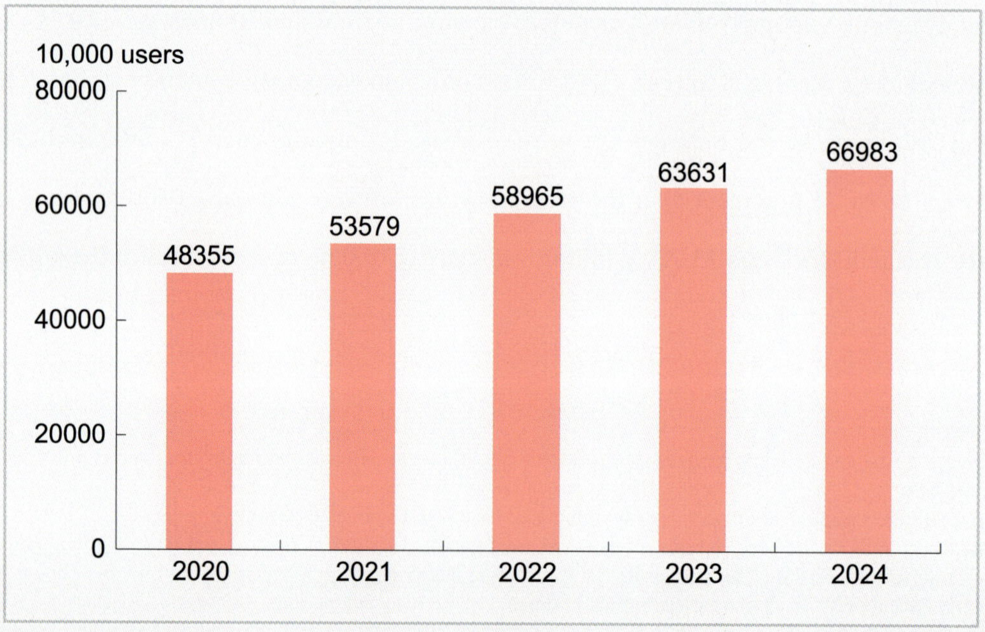

V. Domestic Trade

In 2024, the total retail sales of consumer goods[38] reached 48,334.5 billion yuan, up by 3.5 percent over

37. The statistical coverage of express delivery was adjusted in 2024 and the growth rate was calculated on a comparable basis.
38. The data of the total retail sales of consumer goods were revised in accordance with the results of the Fifth National Economic Census.

the previous year. An analysis on different areas showed that the retail sales of consumer goods in urban areas stood at 41,781.3 billion yuan, up by 3.4 percent, and that in rural areas reached 6,553.1 billion yuan, up by 4.3 percent. Grouped by consumption patterns, the retail sales of goods were 42,716.5 billion yuan, up by 3.2 percent, and the income of catering industry was 5,618.0 billion yuan, up by 5.3 percent. The retail sales of services[39] increased by 6.2 percent over the previous year.

Figure 14: Total Retail Sales of Consumer Goods and Growth Rates 2020-2024

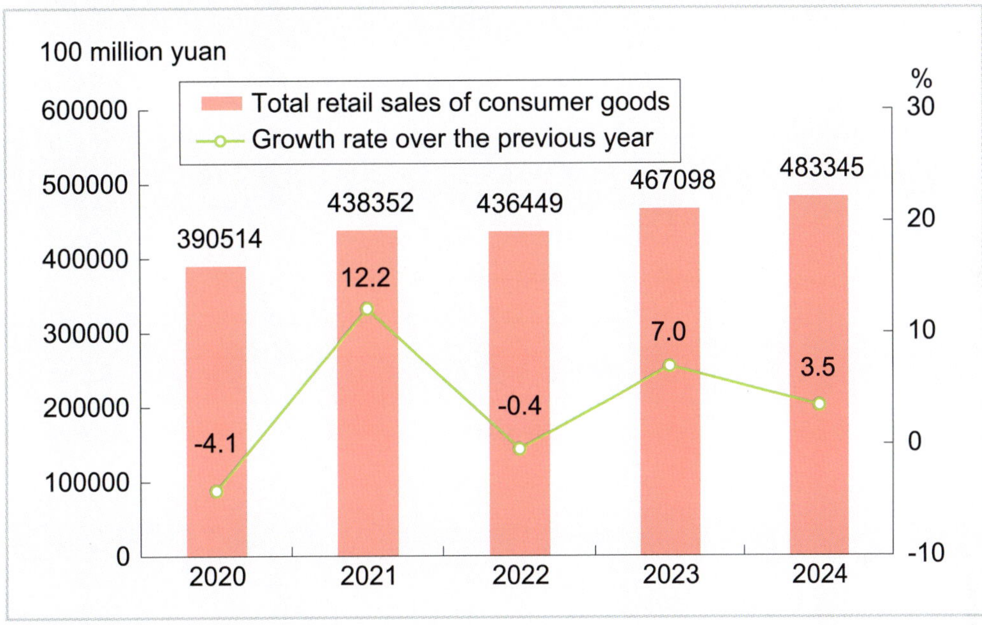

Of the total retail sales of goods by enterprises above the designated size, the retail sales for grain, oil and food went up by 9.9 percent over the previous year; beverage up by 2.1 percent; tobacco and liquor up by 5.7 percent; clothes, shoes, hats and textiles up by 0.3 percent; cosmetics down by 1.1 percent; gold, silver and jewelry down by 3.1 percent; daily necessities up by 3.0 percent; sports and recreational articles up by 11.1 percent; household appliances and audio-video equipment up by 12.3 percent; traditional Chinese and western medicines up by 3.1 percent; cultural and office appliances down by 0.3 percent; furniture up by 3.6 percent; communication equipment up by 9.9 percent; petroleum and petroleum products up by 0.3 percent; motor vehicles down by 0.5 percent; and building and decoration materials down by 2.0 percent. Grouped by retail forms, among all the retail enterprises above the designated size, the retail sales of convenience stores

39. The retail sales of services refer to the total value of services directly provided by enterprises (establishments, self-employed units) to individuals and other units for non-production and non-operating purposes in the form of transactions. It aims to reflect the value of services with the nature of consumption sold by service providers in monetary terms, including the retail sales of services in transportation, accommodation, catering, education, health, sports, entertainment and other fields.

increased by 4.7 percent over the previous year, specialty stores grew by 4.2 percent, supermarkets increased by 2.7 percent, department stores down by 2.4 percent, and brand stores down by 0.4 percent.

In 2024, the online retail sales of physical goods[40] were 12,787.8 billion yuan, up by 6.5 percent over the previous year, accounting for 26.5 percent of the total retail sales of consumer goods.

VI. Investment in Fixed Assets

The total investment in fixed assets of the country in 2024 was 52,091.6 billion yuan, up by 3.1 percent over the previous year[41]. The investment in fixed assets (excluding rural households) was 51,437.4 billion yuan, up by 3.2 percent, among which the investment in purchase of equipment and instruments increased by 15.7 percent. Of the investment in fixed assets (excluding rural households), by region[42], the investment in eastern region was up by 1.3 percent, central region up by 5.0 percent, western region up by 2.4 percent, and northeastern region up by 4.2 percent.

Of the investment in fixed assets (excluding rural households), the investment in the primary industry was 954.3 billion yuan, up by 2.6 percent over the previous year; that in the secondary industry was 17,906.4 billion yuan, up by 12.0 percent; and that in the tertiary industry was 32,576.7 billion yuan, down by 1.1 percent. The investment in infrastructure[43] increased by 4.4 percent. The investment in social sector[44] went down by 2.5 percent. The private investment[45] was 25,757.4 billion yuan, down by 0.1 percent; the private project investment increased by 6.0 percent with the investment in real estate development deducted. By sectors, the private investment in manufacturing increased by 10.8 percent and in infrastructure increased by 5.8 percent.

40. See Note 19.

41. Due to the methodology reform of investment statistics, the revision of data based on the results of the Fifth National Economic Census, the statistical law enforcement and other factors, the growth rates of relevant indicators of investment in fixed assets in 2024 were calculated on a comparable basis.

42. See Note 20.

43. Investment in infrastructure includes investment in railway transportation, highway transportation, waterway transportation, civil aviation transportation, pipeline transportation, multi-modal transportation and forwarding agency, loading, unloading and delivery, postal service, telecommunication, radio, TV and satellite transmission, internet and related services, management of water conservancy, ecological conservation and environmental governance, and management of public facilities.

44. Investment in social sector includes investment in education, health and social services, culture, sports and entertainment.

45. Private investment refers to investment in the construction or purchase of fixed assets in the country by domestic collective, private and individual-owned survey units or their holding units (including absolute holding and relative holding).

Figure 15: Shares of Investment in Fixed Assets (Excluding Rural Households) of the Three Industries in 2024

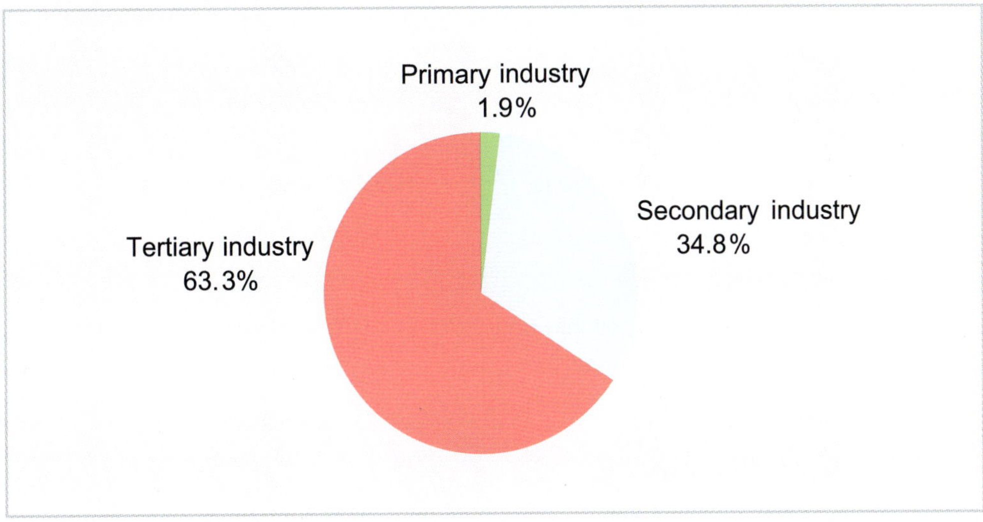

Table 7: Growth Rates of Investment in Fixed Assets (Excluding Rural Households) by Sectors in 2024

Sector	Increase over 2023 (%)	Sector	Increase over 2023 (%)
Total	**3.2**	Finance	-6.3
Agriculture, Forestry, Animal Husbandry and Fishery	6.4	Real Estate[46]	-10.8
Mining	10.5	Leasing and Business Services	6.3
Manufacturing	9.2	Scientific Research and Technical Services	11.8
Production and Supply of Electricity, Heat Power, Gas and Water	23.9	Management of Water Conservancy, Environment and Public Facilities	4.2
Construction	-1.9	Household Services, Repair and Other Services	0.7
Wholesale and Retail Trades	5.0	Education	1.3
Transport, Storage and Post	5.9	Health and Social Services	-9.4
Hotels and Catering Services	34.1	Culture, Sports and Entertainment	0.0
Information Transmission, Software and Information Technology Services	6.3	Public Management, Social Security and Social Organizations	-4.2

46. The investment in real estate includes the investment in real estate development, construction of buildings for own use, property management, intermediary services and other real estate investment.

Table 8: Newly Increased Production and Operation Capacity through Fixed Assets Investment in 2024

Item	Unit	Volume
Newly increased alternating current transformer equipment with a capacity of over 220 kilovolts	10,000 kilovolt-amperes	32119
New railways put into operation	kilometer	3113
Of which: high-speed railways	kilometer	2457
Extended or new double-track railways put into operation	kilometer	2687
Electrified railways put into operation	kilometer	3936
Length of new and rebuilt highways	kilometer	8968
New throughput capacity of berths for over 10,000-tonnage ships	10,000 tons/year	27106
New civil transportation airports	-	4
New lines of optical-fiber cables	10,000 km	856

In 2024, the investment in real estate development was 10,028.0 billion yuan, down by 10.6 percent over the previous year[47]. Of this total, the investment in residential buildings reached 7,604.0 billion yuan, a decrease of 10.5 percent, that in office buildings was 416.0 billion yuan, down by 9.0 percent, and that in buildings for commercial business was 694.4 billion yuan, down by 13.9 percent. In 2024, the floor space of newly-built commercial buildings sold[48] was 973.85 million square meters. The floor space of second-hand housing online transactions[49] reached 718.12 million square meters. The floor space of newly-built commercial buildings for sale was 753.27 million square meters at the end of 2024, among which the floor space of the commercial residential buildings for sale was 390.88 million square meters.

47. The historical data of indicators such as real estate development and sales of newly-built commercial buildings were revised in accordance with the results of the Fifth National Economic Census. The growth rates of 2024 were calculated on a comparable basis.

48. The floor space of newly-built commercial buildings sold refers to the total contract floor space of newly-built commercial buildings sold by real estate development enterprises within the reporting period.

49. The floor space of second-hand housing online transactions refers to the total contract floor space of second-hand housing online transactions in urban areas within the reporting period.

Table 9: Main Indicators for Real Estate Development and Sales and Growth Rates in 2024

Item	Unit	Volume	Increase over 2023 (%)
Investment in real estate development	100 million RMB	100280	-10.6
Of which: residential buildings	100 million RMB	76040	-10.5
Floor space of buildings under construction	10000 square meters	733247	-12.7
Of which: residential buildings	10000 square meters	513330	-13.1
Floor space of buildings newly started	10000 square meters	73893	-23.0
Of which: residential buildings	10000 square meters	53660	-23.0
Floor space of buildings completed	10000 square meters	73743	-27.7
Of which: residential buildings	10000 square meters	53741	-27.4
Floor space of newly-built commercial buildings sold	10000 square meters	97385	-12.9
Of which: residential buildings	10000 square meters	81450	-14.1
Funds for investment this year of real estate development enterprises	100 million RMB	107661	-17.0
Of which: domestic loans	100 million RMB	15217	-6.1
individual mortgage	100 million RMB	15661	-27.9

In 2024, 1.80 million units of government-subsidized housing for sale, government-subsidized rental housing and public rental housing were started to be built or made available; 1.89 million units of resettlement housing for urban village renovation were started to be built or made available, 79 thousand units of dilapidated housing in urban areas were started to be renovated; 58 thousand old urban residential communities were newly started to be renovated, benefiting 9.66 million households; renovation on dilapidated housing and for earthquake resistance of housing in rural areas were started for 239 thousand households, targeting key groups such as low-income rural population.

VII. Foreign Economic Relations

The total value of imports and exports of goods in 2024 reached 43,846.8 billion yuan, up by 5.0 percent over that of the previous year. Of this total, the value of goods exported was 25,454.5 billion yuan, up by 7.1 percent; the value of goods imported was 18,392.3 billion yuan, up by 2.3 percent. The surplus of trade in goods reached 7,062.3 billion yuan. The total value of imports and exports between China and countries along the Belt and Road[50] was 22,068.5 billion yuan, an increase of 6.4 percent over that of the previous year. Of this total, the value of exports was 12,209.5 billion yuan, up by 9.6 percent; the value of imports was 9,858.9 billion yuan, up by 2.7 percent. The total value of imports and exports between China and other Regional Comprehensive Economic Partnership (RCEP) member countries[51] was 13,164.5 billion yuan, up by 4.5 percent over that of the previous year. The total value of imports and exports by private enterprises was 24,332.9 billion yuan, up by 8.8 percent over that of the previous year, accounting for 55.5 percent of the total value of imports and exports. Of this total, the value of exports was 16,471.7 billion yuan, up by 9.4 percent.

Figure 16: Total Value of Imports and Exports of Goods 2020-2024

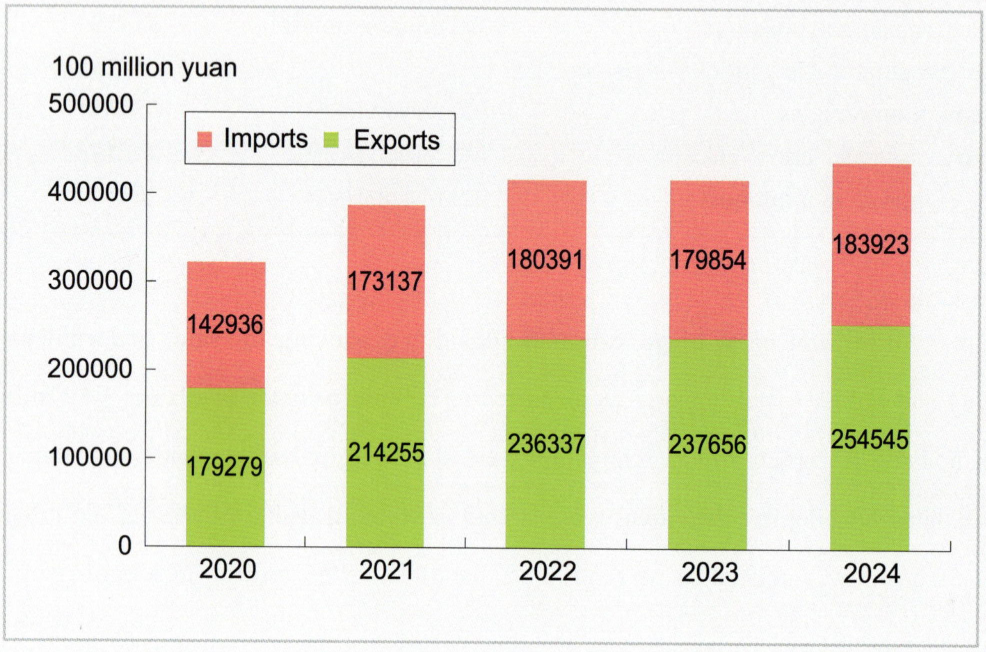

50. The Belt and Road refers to the Silk Road Economic Belt and the 21st Century Maritime Silk Road.

51. Other Regional Comprehensive Economic Partnership (RCEP) member countries include Indonesia, Malaysia, Philippines, Thailand, Singapore, Brunei, Cambodia, Laos, Myanmar, Vietnam, Japan, Republic of Korea, Australia and New Zealand.

Table 10: Total Value and Growth Rates of Imports and Exports of Goods in 2024

Item	Value (100 million yuan)	Increase over 2023 (%)
Total value of imports and exports of goods	**438468**	**5.0**
Exports	254545	7.1
Of which: General trade	166466	8.5
Processing trade	50201	2.4
Of which: Mechanical and electronic products	151246	8.7
High & new technology products	62792	6.0
Imports	183923	2.3
Of which: General trade	114827	-1.9
Processing trade	28920	7.0
Of which: Mechanical and electronic products	70095	7.3
High & new technology products	53584	11.9
Trade surplus in goods	**70623**	**22.2**

Table 11: Volume and Value of Main Export Commodities and the Growth Rates in 2024

Item	Unit	Volume	Increase over 2023 (%)	Value (100 million yuan)	Increase over 2023 (%)
Rolled steel	10000 tons	11072	22.7	5950	0.4
Textile yarns and textile articles	—	—	—	10102	7.0
Clothes and clothing accessories	—	—	—	11326	1.4
Footwear	10000 pairs	920152	3.3	3336	-3.8
Furniture and parts	—	—	—	4830	7.0
Luggage and similar containers	10000 tons	362	9.6	2458	-2.0
Toys	—	—	—	2837	-0.7
Plastic articles	—	—	—	7549	6.7
Integrated circuits	100 million pieces	2981	11.6	11352	18.7
Automatic data processing machines and components	—	—	—	14661	11.2
Mobile phones	10000 sets	81394	1.5	9559	-2.4
Containers	10000 units	545	135.7	1213	108.6
Liquid crystal display modules	10000 units	189264	11.9	2066	10.3
Motor vehicles (including chassis)	10000 sets	641	22.8	8347	16.5

Table 12: Volume and Value of Main Import Commodities and the Growth Rates in 2024

Item	Unit	Volume	Increase over 2023 (%)	Value (100 million yuan)	Increase over 2023 (%)
Soybean	10000 tons	10503	6.5	3751	-9.8
Edible vegetable oil	10000 tons	716	-26.8	528	-27.9
Iron ore and concentrate	10000 tons	123655	4.9	9406	-1.4
Coal and lignite	10000 tons	54270	14.4	3705	-0.7
Crude oil	10000 tons	55342	-1.9	23108	-2.7
Petroleum products refined	10000 tons	4823	1.0	2083	5.7
Natural gas	10000 tons	13169	9.9	4637	2.5
Plastics in primary forms	10000 tons	2898	-2.1	3117	-2.0
Paper pulp	10000 tons	3435	-6.3	1593	-4.3
Rolled steel	10000 tons	681	-10.9	819	-8.1
Unwrought copper and its alloys	10000 tons	568	3.4	3848	14.7
Integrated circuits	100 million pieces	5492	14.6	27445	11.7
Motor vehicles (including chassis)	10000 sets	71	-11.7	2785	-16.1

Table 13: Imports and Exports of Goods with Major Countries and Regions, Growth Rates and Proportions in 2024

Country or region	Exports (100 million yuan)	Increase over 2023 (%)	Proportion of the total (%)	Imports (100 million yuan)	Increase over 2023 (%)	Proportion of the total (%)
ASEAN	41736	13.4	16.4	28163	3.2	15.3
European Union	36751	4.3	14.4	19164	-3.3	10.4
United States	37337	6.1	14.7	11641	1.2	6.3
Republic of Korea	10415	-0.5	4.1	12931	13.6	7.0
Hong Kong, China	20719	7.3	8.1	1321	37.8	0.7
Japan	10816	-2.3	4.2	11119	-1.7	6.0
Taiwan, China	5350	11.0	2.1	15498	10.5	8.4
Russia	8212	5.0	3.2	9198	1.0	5.0
Brazil	5128	23.3	2.0	8258	-4.4	4.5
India	8574	3.6	3.4	1280	-1.7	0.7
South Africa	1552	-6.5	0.6	2180	-3.0	1.2

The total value of imports and exports of services in 2024 was 7,523.8 billion yuan, up by 14.4 percent over that of the previous year. The export value of services was 3,175.6 billion yuan, up by 18.2 percent. The import value of services was 4,348.2 billion yuan, up by 11.8 percent. The trade deficit in imports and exports of services was 1,172.7 billion yuan.

The year 2024 witnessed the new establishment of 59,080 foreign-invested enterprises, up by 9.9 percent over that of the previous year, and the foreign investment actually utilized totaled 826.3 billion yuan, down by 27.1 percent, or 116.2 billion US dollars, down by 28.8 percent. Specifically, a total of 17,172 enterprises were newly established with investment from countries along the Belt and Road (including investment in China via free ports), up by 23.8 percent; and the direct foreign investment in China reached 114.7 billion yuan, down by 6.2 percent, or 16.1 billion US dollars, down by 8.4 percent. The foreign investment actually utilized by high technology industry reached 286.4 billion yuan, down by 32.3 percent, or 40.3 billion US dollars, down by 34.0 percent.

Table 14: Total Value of Foreign Direct Investment and the Growth Rates in 2024

Sector	Enterprises	Increase over 2023 (%)	Actually Utilized Value (100 million yuan)	Increase over 2023 (%)
Total	**59080**	**9.9**	**8263**	**-27.1**
Of which: Agriculture, Forestry, Animal Husbandry and Fishery	374	-10.5	27	-46.0
Manufacturing	3871	6.8	2212	-30.4
Production and Supply of Electricity, Heat Power, Gas and Water	439	-22.7	284	-10.9
Transport, Storage and Post	838	-3.3	112	-25.0
Information Transmission, Software and Information Technology Services	3988	6.0	526	-53.6
Wholesale and Retail	20854	15.8	584	-15.4
Real Estate	612	-10.5	406	-49.9
Leasing and Business Services	11158	4.5	1815	-0.2
Household Services, Repair and Other Services	859	18.3	35	3.6

In 2024, the non-financial outbound direct investment reached 1,024.5 billion yuan, up by 11.7 percent over that of the previous year, or 143.8 billion US dollars, up by 10.5 percent. Of this total, the investment to countries along the Belt and Road reached 239.9 billion yuan, up by 6.5 percent, or 33.7 billion US dollars, up by 5.4 percent.

Table 15: Total Value and Growth Rates of Non-financial Outbound Direct Investment in 2024

Sector	Value (100 million US dollars)	Increase over 2023 (%)
Total	**1438**	**10.5**
Of which: Agriculture, Forestry, Animal Husbandry and Fishery	14	72.0
Mining	125	80.1
Manufacturing	296	6.2
Production and Supply of Electricity, Heat Power, Gas and Water	64	109.5
Construction	40	-40.0
Wholesale and Retail	282	-3.6
Transport, Storage and Post	74	13.7
Information Transmission, Software and Information Technology Services	58	18.8
Real Estate	17	66.5
Leasing and Business Services	404	19.9

In 2024, the accomplished business revenue through contracted overseas engineering projects was 1,182.0 billion yuan, up by 4.2 percent over that of the previous year, or 166.0 billion US dollars, up by 3.1 percent. Specifically, the accomplished business revenue from countries along the Belt and Road was 138.8 billion US dollars, up by 3.4 percent, accounting for 83.6 percent of the accomplished business revenue through contracted overseas engineering projects. The number of labor forces sent abroad through overseas labor contracts was 0.41 million.

VIII. Finance

The national general public budget revenue reached 21,970.2 billion yuan in 2024, up by 1.3 percent over that of the previous year, of which the tax revenue amounted to 17,497.2 billion yuan, down by 3.4 percent. The national general public budget expenditure reached 28,461.2 billion yuan, up by 3.6 percent over that of the previous year. The current main policies supporting sci-tech innovation and the development of manufacturing saw the tax cuts, fee reductions and tax refunds totaling 2,629.3 billion yuan in 2024.

Figure 17: National General Public Budget Revenue 2020-2024

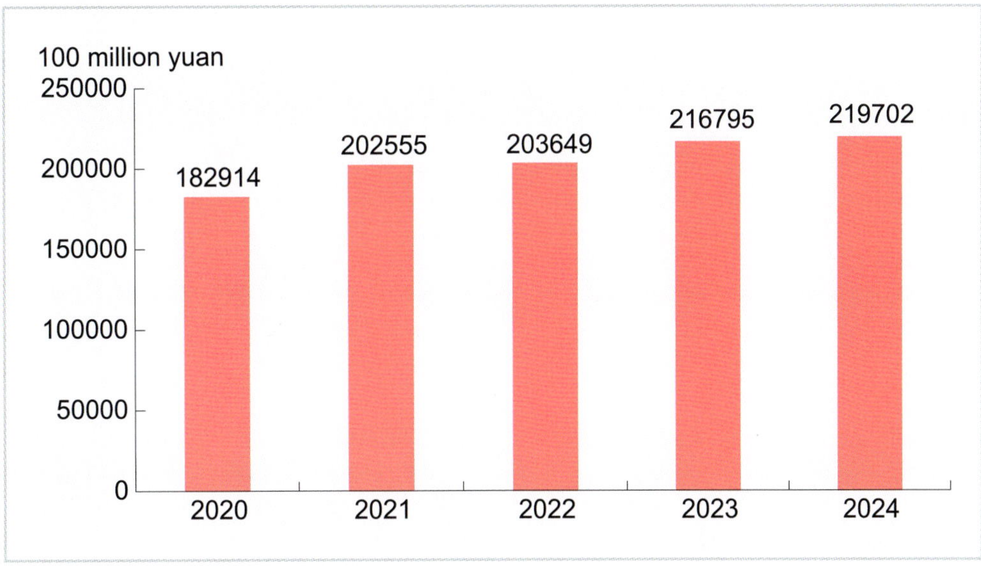

Note: Data for general public budget revenue from 2020 to 2023 as shown in the figure were final accounts and that of 2024 was the executive accounts.

By the end of 2024, money supply of broad sense (M_2) was 313.5 trillion yuan, an increase of 7.3 percent over that by the end of the previous year. Money supply of narrow sense (M_1) was 67.1 trillion yuan, down by 1.4 percent. Cash in circulation (M_0) was 12.8 trillion yuan, up by 13.0 percent.

In 2024, the aggregate financing to the real economy (AFRE) (flow)[52] reached 32.3 trillion yuan, or 3.3 trillion yuan less than that in 2023 on a comparable basis. The AFRE (stock)[53] totaled 408.3 trillion yuan at the end of 2024, up by 8.0 percent over that at the end of 2023 on a comparable basis. Specifically, loans granted to the real economy in Renminbi stood at 252.5 trillion yuan, up by 7.2 percent. Savings deposit in Renminbi and foreign currencies in all items of financial institutions totaled 308.4 trillion yuan at the end of 2024, an increase of 18.5 trillion yuan compared with that at the beginning of the year. Of this total, the savings deposit in Renminbi stood at 302.3 trillion yuan, an increase of 18.0 trillion yuan. Loans in Renminbi and foreign currencies in all items of financial institutions reached 259.6 trillion yuan, an increase of 17.3 trillion yuan. Of this total, loans in Renminbi were 255.7 trillion yuan, an increase of 18.1 trillion yuan. Inclusive loans to micro and small businesses in Renminbi[54] reached 32.9 trillion yuan, an increase of 4.2

52. The AFRE (flow) refers to the total volume of financing provided by the financial system to the real economy within a certain period of time.

53. The AFRE (stock) refers to the outstanding financing provided by the financial system to the real economy at the end of a period of time (a month, a quarter or a year).

54. Inclusive loans to micro and small businesses include loans to micro and small businesses with single-client credit line under 10 million yuan, operating loans to self-employed businesses and owners of micro and small businesses.

trillion yuan. Loans to agriculture, rural areas and rural residents[55] in Renminbi and foreign currencies were 51.4 trillion yuan, an increase of 4.7 trillion yuan. Medium and long-term loans to the manufacturing sector in Renminbi reached 14.0 trillion yuan, an increase of 1.6 trillion yuan. Green loans were 36.6 trillion yuan, an increase of 6.5 trillion yuan.

Table 16: Savings Deposit and Loans in RMB and Foreign Currencies in All Financial Institutions and the Growth Rates at the End of 2024

Item	Year-end figure (100 million yuan)	Increase over 2023 (%)
Savings deposit	**3083849**	**6.4**
Domestic households	1522529	10.4
Deposits in RMB	1512509	10.4
Domestic non-financial enterprises	814791	-0.4
Loans	**2595750**	**7.2**
Domestic short-term loans	653951	5.0
Domestic medium- and long-term loans	1713857	7.7

Loans in Renminbi from rural financial institutions (rural credit cooperatives, rural cooperation banks and rural commercial banks) totaled 31.5 trillion yuan by the end of 2024, an increase of 2.1 trillion yuan as compared with that at the beginning of the year. Consumption loans in Renminbi from all financial institutions totaled 58.7 trillion yuan, an increase of 0.7 trillion yuan. Of the total, household short-term consumption loans totaled 10.2 trillion yuan, a decrease of 0.2 trillion yuan, and household medium and long-term consumption loans reached 48.5 trillion yuan, an increase of 0.9 trillion yuan.

Funds raised through A-shares issued on Shanghai and Shenzhen Stock Exchanges[56] amounted to 425.1 billion yuan in 2024, a decrease of 648.4 billion yuan from the previous year. A total of 77 new A-shares issued on Shanghai and Shenzhen Stock Exchanges raised 62.2 billion yuan worth of capital altogether, down by 279.6 billion yuan over that of the previous year. Of the total, 15 shares issued on the Science and Technology Innovation Board raised 15.2 billion yuan; refinancing of A-shares on Shanghai and Shenzhen Stock Exchanges (including public offerings, private placements, right issues, preferred shares and conversions of convertible bonds) raised 362.9 billion yuan, a decrease of 368.8 billion yuan over that of

55. From June 2024, the statistical coverage of rural areas has been adjusted with the urban areas of a county being removed from rural areas. Figures of loans to agriculture, rural areas and rural residents are comparable figures.

56. Funds raised through Shanghai and Shenzhen Stock Exchanges are calculated by the money raised on the listing date, and the funds raised include the actual exchanged convertible bonds, which were 83.2 billion yuan in 2023 and 169.4 billion yuan in 2024.

the previous year. Funds raised through Beijing Stock Exchanges[57] reached 4.8 billion yuan with 23 shares publicly issued. Market entities raised 13.4 trillion yuan through issuing bonds (including corporate bonds, enterprise bonds, asset-backed securities, national and local government bonds) on Shanghai, Shenzhen and Beijing Stock Exchanges. Specifically, 29 Real Estate Investment Trust Funds (REITs) in infrastructure sector were listed on Shanghai and Shenzhen Stock Exchanges, raising 65.5 billion yuan. There were 6,101 companies listed on National Equities Exchange and Quotations and 11.9 billion yuan raised by listed companies[58] in 2024.

In 2024, the issuance of corporate credit bonds[59] reached 14.8 trillion yuan, an increase of 1.0 trillion yuan over that of the previous year.

The premium of primary insurance received by the insurance companies[60] totaled 5,696.3 billion yuan in 2024, up by 5.7 percent over that of the previous year on a comparable basis. Of this total, life insurance premium of primary insurance amounted to 3,191.7 billion yuan, health and casualty insurance premium of primary insurance 1,071.5 billion yuan, and property insurance premium of primary insurance 1,433.1 billion yuan. An indemnity worth of 2,300.5 billion yuan was paid, of which, life insurance indemnity was 874.7 billion yuan, health and casualty insurance indemnity 444.9 billion yuan, and property insurance indemnity 981.0 billion yuan.

IX. Household Income and Consumption and Social Security

In 2024, the per capita disposable income nationwide was 41,314 yuan, an increase of 5.3 percent over that of the previous year or a real increase of 5.1 percent after deducting price factors. The median[61] of per capita disposable income nationwide was 34,707 yuan, up by 5.1 percent. In terms of permanent residence, the per capita disposable income of urban households was 54,188 yuan, up by 4.6 percent over that of 2023, or a real growth of 4.4 percent after deducting price factors. The median of per capita disposable income of urban households was 49,302 yuan, up by 4.6 percent. The per capita disposable income of rural households was 23,119 yuan, up by 6.6 percent over that of the previous year, or 6.3 percent in real terms after deducting

57. Funds raised through Beijing Stock Exchanges are calculated by the money raised on the listing date.

58. Preferred shares were excluded from the funds raised by listed companies in the National Equities Exchange and Quotations. Funds raised by shares are calculated by the disclosure date of the issuance report.

59. Corporate credit bonds include debt financing instruments issued by non-financial businesses, enterprise bonds, corporate bonds and convertible bonds.

60. The premium of primary insurance received by the insurance companies refers to the premium income from primary insurance contracts confirmed by the insurance companies.

61. The median of per capita disposable income refers to the per capita income of household lied in the middle of all surveyed households which are ranked from low to high based on per capita disposable income level.

price factors. The median of per capita disposable income of rural households was 19,605 yuan, up by 4.6 percent. The urban-rural per capita disposable income ratio was 2.34, narrowed by 0.05 over that of the previous year. Grouped by income quintile[62], the per capita disposable income of low-income group reached 9,542 yuan, the lower-middle-income group 21,608 yuan, the middle-income group 33,925 yuan, the upper-middle-income group 53,359 yuan and the high-income group 98,809 yuan. The per capita monthly income of migrant workers was 4,961 yuan, increased by 3.8 percent over that of the previous year. In 2024, the per capita disposable income of rural households from counties lifted out of poverty[63] was 17,522 yuan, up by 6.9 percent over that of 2023, or a real growth of 6.5 percent after deducting price factors.

The national per capita consumption expenditure was 28,227 yuan, up by 5.3 percent over that of the previous year, or a real increase of 5.1 percent after deducting price factors. Specifically, the per capita consumption expenditure on services[64] totaled 13,016 yuan, up by 7.4 percent over that of the previous year, accounting for 46.1 percent of the per capita consumption expenditure. In terms of permanent residence, the per capita consumption expenditure of urban households was 34,557 yuan, up by 4.7 percent, or up by 4.5

Figure 18: National Per Capita Disposable Income and the Growth Rates 2020-2024

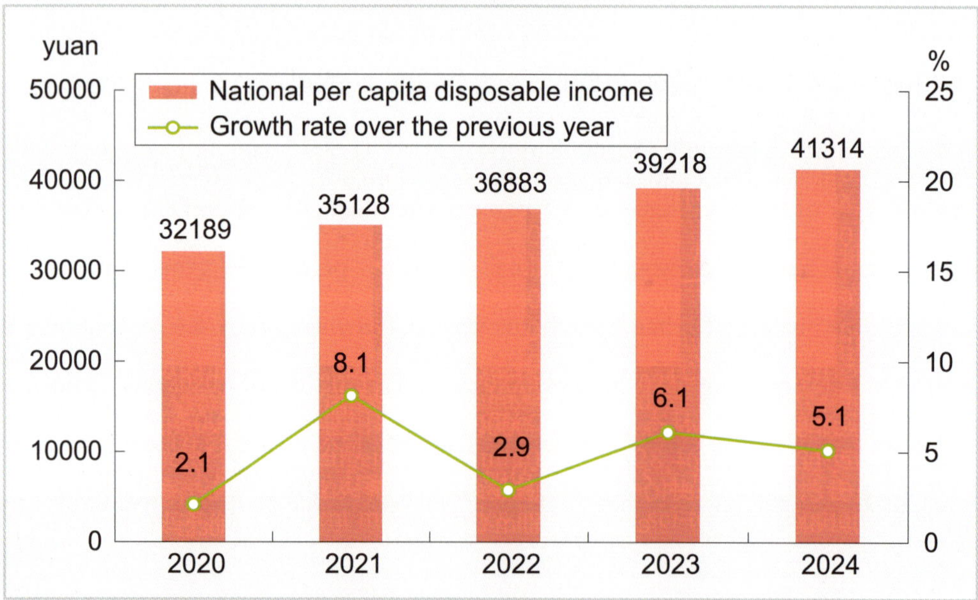

62. The income quintile refers to the five equal partitions of all surveyed households, who are ranked from low to high based on per capita income level. The bottom 20 percent with the lowest income are classified as low-income group, and the other four levels are lower-middle-income group, middle-income group, upper-middle-income group and high-income group.

63. Counties lifted out of poverty include 832 key counties under the national poverty alleviation and development program and counties in contiguous poor areas as well as 7 cities and counties in Aksu prefecture, Xinjiang.

64. The consumption expenditure on services refers to the spending by households on services for daily lives including catering, clothing and footwear processing, housing, family, transportation and communication, education, culture and recreation, medical services and others.

percent in real terms after deducting price factors. The per capita consumption expenditure of rural households was 19,280 yuan, up by 6.1 percent, or a real increase of 5.8 percent after deducting price factors. The national Engel's Coefficient stood at 29.8 percent, with that of urban and rural households standing at 28.8 percent and 32.3 percent respectively.

Figure 19: National Per Capita Consumption Expenditure and Composition in 2024

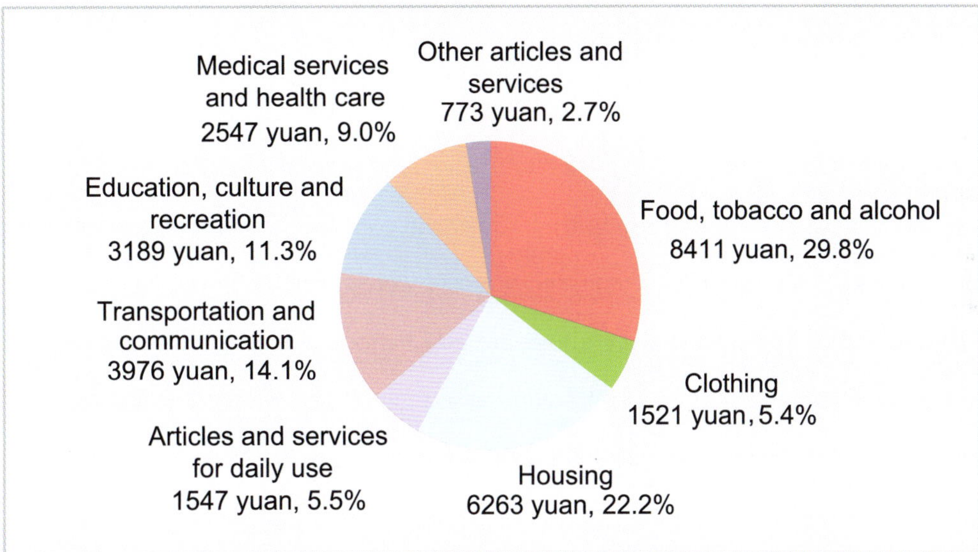

By the end of 2024, a total of 534.49 million people participated in the basic endowment insurance program for urban workers, an increase of 13.29 million over that by the end of 2023. A total of 538.30 million people participated in basic endowment insurance program for urban and rural residents, a decrease of 6.92 million. A total of 1,326.38 million people participated in basic medical insurance program. Of this total, 379.20 million people participated in the program for workers, and 947.18 million people participated in the program for urban and rural residents. A total of 245.89 million people participated in unemployment insurance program, an increase of 2.16 million. A total of 303.98 million people participated in work-related injury insurance, an increase of 2.24 million. A total of 252.98 million people participated in maternity insurance programs. By the end of 2024, minimum living allowances were granted to 6.25 million urban residents and 33.62 million rural residents, 4.39 million rural residents living in extreme poverty[65] received relief and assistance and 7.72 million person-times of temporary assistance[66] were provided. National

65. Rural residents living in extreme poverty refer to the aged, the disabled and the minor under 16 years of age in rural areas who have no ability to work, no sources of income and no statutory obligors to provide for them, bring them up or support them, or whose statutory obligors have no ability to fulfill their obligations.

66. Temporary assistance refers to emergent and transitional assistance provided by the government to families or individuals who experience hardships because of emergencies, unexpected harm, major diseases or other unusual factors and are not covered by other forms of social assistance programs or still suffer hardships after receiving other social assistance programs.

pensions and subsidies were regularly provided to 8.22 million ex-servicemen and other entitled people in 2024.

By the end of 2024, there were altogether 43 thousand social welfare institutions providing accommodation, of which 40 thousand were elderly care institutions and 1,045 were institutions for child welfare, assistance and protection. The social welfare institutions provided 8.253 million beds[67], of which 7.991 million were for the elderly and 97 thousand were for children.

X. Science & Technology and Education

Expenditures on research and experimental development activities (R&D) were 3,613.0 billion yuan in 2024, up by 8.3 percent over that of 2023, accounting for 2.68 percent of GDP. Of this total, 249.7 billion yuan was used for basic research programs, up by 10.5 percent over that of 2023, accounting for 6.91 percent of expenditures on R&D. A total of 54.9 thousand projects were financed by the National Natural Science Foundation. By the end of 2024, there were altogether 206 national engineering research centers included into the new sequence management and 1,798 enterprise technology centers recognized by the National Development and Reform Commission. The National Guiding Fund for Transformation of Scientific and Technological Achievements established 36 sub-funds, with a total funding of 62.4 billion yuan. There were 1,606 state-level technology business incubators[68], and 2,376 national mass makerspaces[69]. A total of 1.045 million invention patents were authorized, up by 13.5 percent over that of the previous year. The number of PCT patent applications accepted[70] was 75 thousand. By the end of 2024, the number of valid invention patents was 5.689 million, up by 14.0 percent over that by the end of 2023. The number of high-value invention patents per 10,000 people[71] was 14. Trademark registration totaled 4.781 million, up by 9.1 percent over that of the previous year. A total of 0.99 million technology contracts were signed with 6,835.4 billion

67. The beds provided by social welfare institutions include beds provided by adoption agencies, aid agencies and community agencies.

68. The state-level technology business incubators are technology-based business start-up service providers consistent with the Administrative Measures for Technology Business Incubators that provide physical space, shared facilities and professional services with the mission of advancing transformation of technological achievements, cultivating technological enterprises and fostering the entrepreneurial spirit. They should be approved and accredited by the Ministry of Science and Technology.

69. The national mass makerspaces are new service platform for entrepreneurship and innovation that are in conformity with the Guidelines on Developing Mass Makerspaces and are reviewed and registered by the Ministry of Science and Technology in accordance with the Provisional Registration Regulations on National Mass Makerspaces.

70. The number of PCT patent applications accepted refers to the number of PCT patent application accepted by the State Intellectual Property Office which acts as the receiving office of PCT patent application. PCT is the abbreviation of Patent Cooperation Treaty, which is a treaty for international cooperation in the field of patents.

71. The number of high-value invention patents per 10,000 people refers to the number of valid invention patents owned per 10,000 national residents which are authorized by the China National Intellectual Property Administration and satisfy any of the following conditions: invention patents for strategic emerging industries; invention patents having corresponding foreign patents; invention patents maintained more than 10 years; invention patents with a relatively high pledge financing amount; and invention patents that won the National Science and Technology Award and the China Patent Award.

yuan worth of contracted technology transactions, up by 11.2 percent over that of the previous year. The proportion of citizens with scientific literacy[72] in China reached 15.37 percent.

Figure 20: Expenditure on Research and Experimental Development Activities (R&D) and the Growth Rates 2020-2024

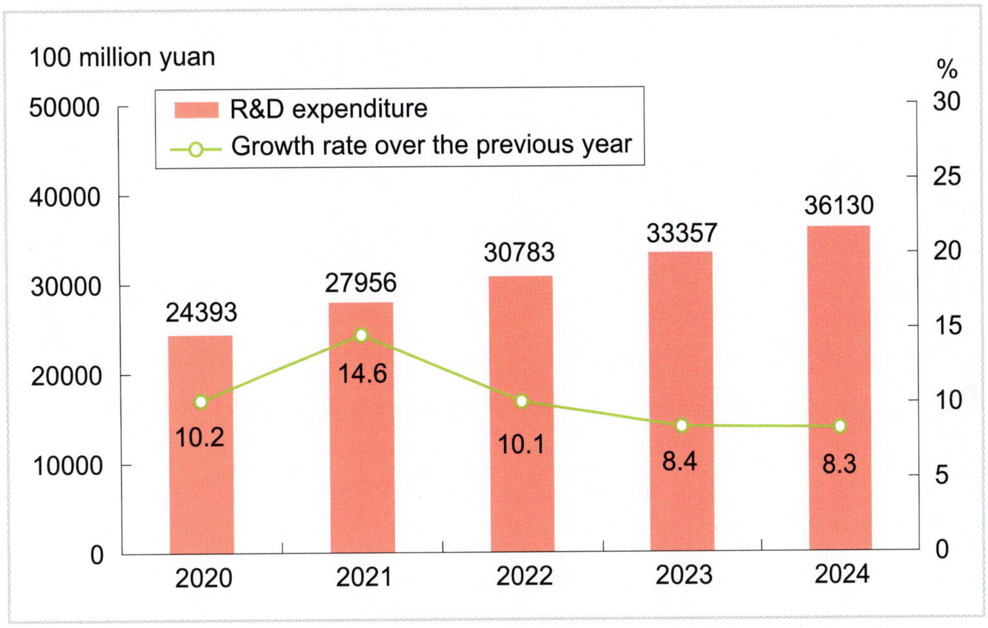

Table 17: Number of Patents Authorized and Valid Patents in 2024

Item	Patents (10,000)	Increase over 2023 (%)
Number of invention patents authorized	104.5	13.5
Of which: domestic	93.2	14.6
Number of utility model patents authorized	201.0	-3.9
Number of appearance design patents authorized	64.3	0.8
Number of valid invention patents at the end of the year	568.9	14.0
Of which: domestic	468.2	16.6
Number of valid utility model patents at the end of the year	1165.7	-3.9
Number of valid appearance design patents at the end of the year	307.4	-4.9

72. Citizens with scientific literacy refer to citizens carrying out scientific spirit, spreading scientific philosophy, mastering basic scientific methods and scientific knowledge, and able to apply them to analysis and problem solving. The proportion of citizens with scientific literacy was obtained from the sample survey for citizens aged from 18 to 69.

The year 2024 saw a total of 68 successful space launches. China's Chang'e-6 spacecraft successfully brought back the first samples from the far side of the Moon. The first reusable and returnable test satellite was successfully retrieved. The number of pulsars discovered by China's Five-hundred-meter Aperture Spherical Radio Telescope (FAST) has exceeded 1,000. The world's first high-definition geologic atlas of the whole Moon was officially released. The plasma current of China's HL-3 tokamak exceeded 1.5 MA. A quantum simulator that outperforms classical computers was successfully constructed for the first time. A new-generation meteorological supercomputer system was launched. China's first domestically designed and built deep-ocean drilling vessel called "Meng Xiang" was officially commissioned. A new-generation medium-sized multi-role stealth fighter jet made its debut at the 15th China International Aviation and Aerospace Exhibition.

By the end of 2024, there were altogether 874 national quality inspection centers. There were 1,230 agencies for product quality, management system and service certification which certified accumulatively 1.10 million enterprises. A total of 3,154 national standards were developed or revised in the year, including 2,001 new standards. The qualification rate of manufactured products[73] reached 93.93 percent.

In 2024, graduate institutes enrolled 4.095 million students with 1.357 million entrants and 1.084 million graduates. Total enrollment in undergraduate programs in regular and vocational higher education institutes[74] was 38.913 million with 10.689 million entrants and 10.594 million graduates. The enrollment in secondary vocational education[75] was 16.594 million with 5.754 million entrants and 5.422 million graduates. Regular senior secondary schools had 29.223 million enrolled students, including 10.362 million entrants and 8.910 million graduates. Students enrolled in junior secondary schools totaled 53.862 million, including 18.488 million entrants and 16.982 million graduates. The country had a primary education enrollment of 105.844 million, including 16.166 million entrants and 18.573 million graduates. There were 0.916 million students enrolled in special education schools, with 0.158 million entrants and 0.177 million graduates. Kindergartens accommodated 35.840 million children. The retention rate in nine-year compulsory education reached 95.9 percent, and the gross enrollment ratio for senior secondary education reached 92.0 percent.

73. The qualification rate of manufactured products is the ratio of the samples that have passed the sampling quality test, the process of which follows certain methods, procedure and standard, to the total amount of the sampled products. The survey samples cover 29 sectors of the manufacturing industry.

74. Regular and vocational higher education institutes include regular universities, vocational undergraduate education and higher vocational colleges.

75. Secondary vocational education includes regular specialized secondary schools, adult specialized secondary schools, vocational high schools and skilled workers schools.

Figure 21: Entrants in Education 2020-2024

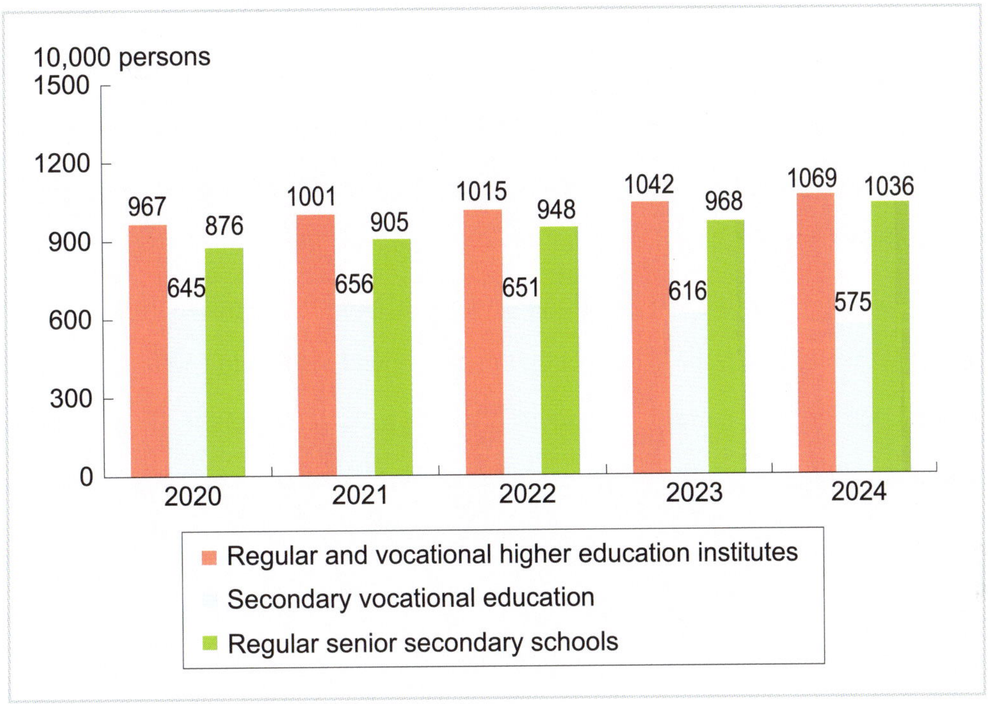

XI. Culture and Tourism, Public Health and Sports

By the end of 2024, there were 1,888 art-performing groups affiliated to government culture and tourism departments throughout China. A total of 3,248 public libraries received[76] 1,341.97 million person-times of visits nationwide. There were 3,516 cultural centers. Subscribers to cable television programs numbered 209 million, among which 201 million subscribed to digital cable television programs. By the end of 2024, radio broadcasting and television program coverage rates were 99.7 percent and 99.8 percent respectively. A total of 3,490 episodes of 115 TV series and 108,271 minutes of TV cartoons were produced in 2024. The country developed 612 feature movies and 261 popular science movies, documentaries, animation and special movies[77]. A total of 24.9 billion copies of newspapers and 1.8 billion copies of magazines were issued, and 11.8 billion copies of books were published. The average number of books possessed per person[78] was 8.39 copies. By the end of the year, there were 4,174 archives in China and 252.38 million files were accessible to the public. The business revenue of enterprises above the designated size engaged in culture and related industries reached 14,151.0 billion yuan, up by 6.0 percent over that of the previous year on a comparable basis.

76. The people received by the public libraries refer to the number of people who visit libraries and use library services in the year, including borrowing and reading books, consultation and attending readers' programs.

77. Special movies refer to those using different display modes in terms of projection techniques, equipment and program as compared with the ordinary cinemas, such as IMAX movies, 3D movies, 4D movies, multidimensional movies and full dome movies.

78. The average number of books possessed per person refers to the average number of books published in the year that can be possessed per person in China.

In 2024, a total of 5.62 billion domestic trips were made, up by 14.8 percent over that of the previous year. Of this total, the number of trips made by urban residents was 4.37 billion, an increase of 16.3 percent; and the number of trips made by rural residents was 1.25 billion, an increase of 9.9 percent. The expenditure of domestic tourists was 5,754.3 billion yuan, an increase of 17.1 percent. Of this total, tourists from urban areas spent 4,929.3 billion yuan, an increase of 18.0 percent; and tourists from rural areas spent 825.0 billion yuan, an increase of 12.2 percent. The number of inbound visits to China totaled 131.90 million, up by 60.8 percent. Of this total, 26.94 million were made by foreigners and 104.96 million by Chinese compatriots from Hong Kong, Macao and Taiwan. The expenditures of inbound visitors to China totaled 94.2 billion US dollars, up by 77.8 percent. The number of inbound trips made by foreigners to China under the visa-free policies totaled 20.12 million, up by 112.3 percent. The number of China's outbound visits totaled 145.89 million. Of this total, 140.15 million were private visits and 97.12 million were to Hong Kong, Macao and Taiwan.

Figure 22: Person-times of Domestic Tourists and the Growth Rates 2020-2024

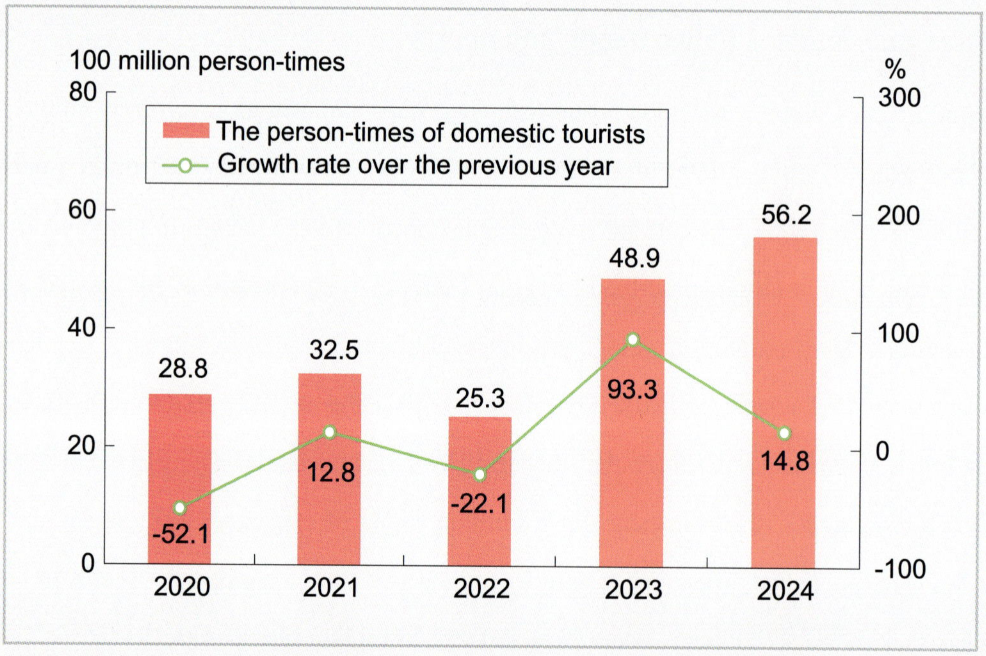

By the end of 2024, there were 1.092 million medical and health institutions in China, including 39 thousand hospitals. Of all the hospitals, 12 thousand were public, and 27 thousand were private. Of the 1.040 million medical and health institutions at grass-root level, 33 thousand were town and township health centers, 37 thousand community health service centers, 398 thousand clinics and 571 thousand village clinics. Of the 9,217 professional public health institutions (excluding health monitoring institutions), 3,429 were disease control and prevention centers. By the end of 2024, there were 12.95 million medical technical personnel in China, including 5.05 million licensed doctors and licensed assistant doctors and 5.84 million registered nurses. The medical and health institutions in China had 10.37 million beds, of which hospitals had 8.18 million and township health centers had 1.51 million. The total number of medical visits[79] and hospital discharges[80] in 2024 reached 10.11 billion and 0.31 billion respectively.

Figure 23: Year-end Number of Medical Technical Personnel 2020-2024

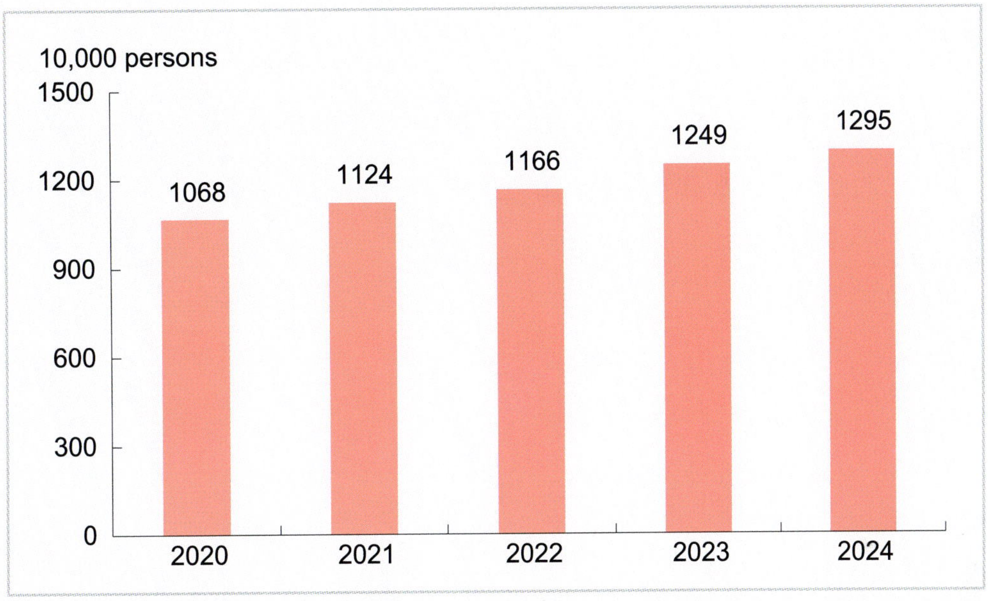

There were altogether 4.842 million sports venues[81]. The sports venue area[82] totaled 4.23 billion square meters and the per capita sports venue area was 3.0 square meters. In 2024, Chinese athletes won 194 world championships in 33 sport competitions and broke 19 world records. At the 33rd Summer Olympic Games, Chinese athletes won 40 gold medals and a total of 91 medals, marking the best performance at an overseas Olympic Games, joint first place in the Olympic gold medal tally and second in the overall medal table. Chinese physically-challenged athletes won 333 world championships in 45 international sport competitions. At the 17th Paralympic Games, Chinese athletes won 94 gold medals and a total of 220 medals, topping the

79. The total number of medical visits refers to the number of people receiving medical services, including outpatient services, emergency treatment, home visits, appointment-based diagnosis and treatment, health check-up of a specific item, and health consultation and guidance (excluding health lectures and nucleic acid tests).

80. The number of hospital discharges refers to the number of inpatients discharged from hospitals in the reporting period, including those who are discharged from hospitals or transferred to other medical institutions following doctors' advice, discharged from hospitals without doctors' permission, dead or other situations. The number of people who are recovered from family sickbeds is excluded.

81. The sports venues belonging to armed forces and railway system are excluded in the census on sports venues.

82. The sports venue area refers to area used for physical training, sports competitions and physical fitness.

gold medal tally and overall medal count for six times in a row at the Paralympic Games.

XII. Resources, Environment and Emergency Management

In 2024, the total supply of state-owned land for construction use[83] was 606 thousand hectares, a decrease of 19.1 percent over that of the previous year. Of this total, the land supply for industry, mining and warehousing was 155 thousand hectares, down by 11.5 percent; that for real estate[84] was 72 thousand hectares, down by 14.7 percent; and that for infrastructure facilities was 380 thousand hectares, down by 22.5 percent.

The total stock of water resources in 2024 was 3,001.0 billion cubic meters. With an increase of 0.3 percent over 2023, the total water consumption was 592.5 billion cubic meters, of which water consumption for domestic use was up by 1.9 percent, for industrial use down by 0.2 percent, for agricultural use down by 0.7 percent, and the artificial recharge for environmental and ecological use grew by 7.8 percent. Water consumption per 10,000 yuan of GDP[85] was 46 cubic meters, a decline of 4.4 percent. Water consumption per 10,000 yuan of industrial value added was 25 cubic meters, down by 5.6 percent. The per capita water consumption was 421 cubic meters, up by 0.4 percent.

In 2024, the total area of afforestation reached 4.45 million hectares, of which 1.18 million hectares were afforested by manpower, accounting for 26.6 percent of the total. The land area improved by grass plantation[86] was 3.22 million hectares. By the end of 2024, there were 5 national parks. The newly treated land of soil erosion covered an area of 64 thousand square kilometers.

Preliminary estimation indicated that the total energy consumption[87] in 2024 amounted to 5.96 billion tons of standard coal equivalent, up by 4.3 percent over that of 2023. The consumption of coal increased by 1.7 percent; crude oil, down by 1.2 percent; natural gas, up by 7.3 percent; and electric power, up by 6.8 percent. The consumption of coal accounted for 53.2 percent of the total energy consumption, 1.6 percentage points lower than that of 2023, while clean energy consumption, such as natural gas, hydropower, nuclear power, wind power and solar power accounted for 28.6 percent, 2.2 percentage points higher. The comprehensive

83. Total supply of state-owned land for construction use refers to the total amount of state-owned land for construction use with the land-use right transferred, allocated or leased to units or individuals through signed transaction contracts and allocation decisions by the municipal or county governments according to annual land supply plan and in line with relevant laws in the reporting period.

84. Land used for real estate refers to the sum of land used for commercial service and for residence.

85. The water consumption per 10,000 yuan of GDP and water consumption per 10,000 yuan of industrial value added are calculated at prices of 2020.

86. The land area improved by grass plantation refers to the area of grasslands that are ecologically restored through manual grass plantation, aerial grass seeding, the quality improvement of grasslands and fencing enclosure.

87. See Note 25.

energy consumption per unit of calcium carbide by major energy-intensive industrial enterprises went down by 0.8 percent, per unit of synthetic ammonia down by 1.2 percent, per ton of steel down by 0.1 percent and per unit of electrolytic aluminium down by 0.2 percent. The standard coal consumption per kilowatt-hour of thermal power generation decreased by 0.2 percent. According to preliminary estimates, the energy consumption per 10,000 yuan worth of GDP[88] decreased by 3.8 percent over that of the previous year after deducting the consumption of raw materials and non-fossil energy. The trade volume of carbon emission quotas[89] at the China Carbon Emissions Trading Market reached 189 million tons with a turnover totaling 18.11 billion yuan.

Figure 24: Proportion of Clean Energy Consumption in the Total Energy Consumption 2020-2024

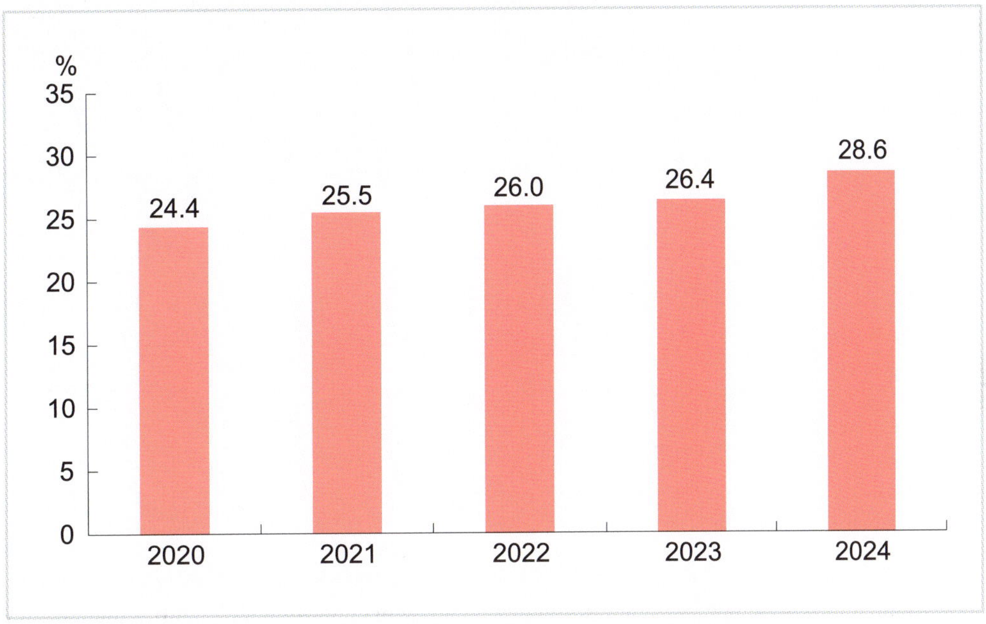

The area of offshore oceanic water[90] that met the national quality standard Grade I and II accounted for 83.7 percent; that met Grade III standard 4.1 percent; and that of Grade IV or inferior quality 12.2 percent.

Of the monitored 339 cities at prefecture level and above, the annual average concentration of particulate matter ($PM_{2.5}$) was 29.3 micrograms per cubic meter, down by 2.7 percent over the previous year.

Of the 326 cities subject to urban regional daytime acoustic environment monitoring, 7.1 percent

88. The energy consumption per 10,000 yuan worth of GDP is calculated at prices of 2020.

89. The carbon emission quotas at the China Carbon Emissions Trading Market refers to the emission quotas of greenhouse gases such as carbon dioxide allocated to major emission entities for the prescribed period at the China Carbon Emissions Trading Market. One unit of carbon emission quota is equivalent to one ton of carbon dioxide equivalent emitted into the atmosphere.

90. Offshore oceanic water quality is evaluated by the area method.

enjoyed excellent environment, 66.9 percent had good environment, 25.5 percent had average environment, 0.6 percent had relatively poor environment and no city had poor environment in 2024.

The average temperature in 2024 was 10.90°C, up by 0.19°C compared with that of the previous year. Typhoons hit China 9 times in 2024.

In 2024, natural disasters hit 10.09 million hectares of crops, of which 1.24 million hectares suffered from complete crop failure. Flood, waterlogging and geological disasters caused a direct economic loss of 263.0 billion yuan. Droughts caused a direct economic loss of 8.4 billion yuan. Disasters caused by low temperature, frost and snow made a direct economic loss of 25.6 billion yuan. Oceanic disasters caused a direct economic loss of 10.9 billion yuan. The country recorded 25 earthquakes with magnitude 5.0 and above, and total direct economic losses of 3.8 billion yuan were caused by earthquakes of different magnitudes. The year 2024 witnessed 292 forest fires, with 7 thousand hectares of forests damaged.

The death toll due to work accidents amounted to 19,626 people in 2024, down by 7.6 percent over that of the previous year. Work accidents in industrial, mining and commercial companies caused 1.089 deaths out of every 100 thousand employees, down by 12.5 percent over that of 2023. The death toll for one million tons of coal produced in coal mines was 0.059 people, down by 37.2 percent. The road traffic death toll per 10 thousand vehicles was 1.31 people, down by 5.1 percent.

Data Sources:

In this Communiqué, data of newly increased employed people in urban areas, endowment insurance, unemployment insurance, work injury insurance and skilled workers schools in secondary vocational education are from the Ministry of Human Resources and Social Security; data of foreign exchange reserves and exchange rates are from the State Administration of Foreign Exchange; data of business entities, quality inspection, the formulation and revision of national standards and qualification rate of manufactured products are from the State Administration for Market Regulation; data of environment quality and carbon emission trading are from the Ministry of Ecology and Environment; data of output of aquatic products are from the Ministry of Agriculture and Rural Affairs; data of production of timber, area of afforestation, area of grass planting and improvement and national parks are from the National Forestry and Grassland Administration; data of installed power generation capacity, newly increased alternating current transformer equipment with a capacity of over 220 kilovolts and electricity consumption are from the China Electricity Council; data of volume of freight handled by ports, container shipping of ports, highway transportation, waterway transportation, new and rebuilt highways and new throughput capacity of berths for over 10,000-tonnage ships are from the Ministry of Transport; data of railway transportation are from the National Railway Administration; data of civil aviation and new civil transportation airports are from the Civil Aviation Administration of China; data of pipeline transportation are from China National Petroleum Corporation, China Petrochemical Corporation, China National Offshore Oil Corporation and China Oil & Gas Piping Network Corporation; data of motor vehicles for civilian use and traffic accidents are from the Ministry of Public Security; data of postal service are from the State Post Bureau; data of telecommunication, software revenue, state-level technology business incubators, national mass makerspaces and technology contracts are from the Ministry of Industry and Information Technology; data of internet users and internet coverage are from the China Internet Network Information Center; data of new railways put into operation, extended or new double-track railways put into operation and electrified railways put into operation are from China Railway; data of floor space of second-hand housing online transactions, government-subsidized housing, urban village renovation, renovation of dilapidated housing in urban areas, renovation of old urban residential communities and renovation of housing in rural areas are from the Ministry of Housing and Urban-Rural Development; data of imports and exports of goods are from the General Administration of

Customs; data of imports and exports of services, newly established foreign-invested enterprises, actually utilized foreign investment, outbound direct investment, overseas contracted projects and overseas labor contracts are from the Ministry of Commerce; data of finance are from the Ministry of Finance; data of tax cuts, fee deductions and tax refunds are from the State Taxation Administration; data of monetary finance and corporate credit bonds are from the People's Bank of China; data of funds raised through domestic exchange markets are from China Securities Regulatory Commission; data of the insurance sector are from the National Financial Regulatory Administration; data of medical insurance and maternity insurance are from the National Healthcare and Security Administration; data of urban and rural minimum living allowances, relief and assistance granted to rural residents living in extreme poverty, temporary assistance and social welfare are from the Ministry of Civil Affairs; data of entitled people are from the Ministry of Veterans Affairs; data of natural science foundation projects are from the National Natural Science Foundation; data of national engineering research centers and enterprise technology centers recognized by the National Development and Reform Commission are from the National Development and Reform Commission; data of National Guiding Fund for Transformation of Scientific and Technological Achievements are from the Ministry of Science and Technology; data of patents and trademarks are from the National Intellectual Property Administration; data of the proportion of citizens with scientific literacy are from the China Association for Science and Technology; data of satellite launches are from the State Administration of Science, Technology and Industry for National Defense; data of education are from the Ministry of Education; data of art-performing groups, public libraries, cultural centers and tourism are from the Ministry of Culture and Tourism; data of television and radio programs are from the National Radio and Television Administration; data of movies are from the China Film Administration; data of newspapers, magazines and books are from the National Press and Publication Administration; data of files are from the State Archives Administration; data of inbound trips made by foreigners to China under the visa-free policies, China's outbound visits are from the National Immigration Administration; data of medical care and health are from the National Health Commission; data of sports are from the General Administration of Sport; data of physically-challenged athletes are from the China Disabled Persons' Federation; data of supply of state-owned land for construction use and direct economic loss caused by oceanic disasters are from the Ministry of Natural Resources; data of stock of water resources, water consumption and newly treated land of soil erosion are from the Ministry of Water Resources; data of average temperature and typhoons are from the China Meteorological Administration; data of areas of crops hit by natural disasters, direct economic loss caused by flood, waterlogging and geological disasters, direct economic loss caused by droughts, direct economic loss caused by low temperature, frost and snow, the number of earthquakes, direct economic losses caused by earthquakes of different magnitudes, forest fires, areas of forests damaged and workplace accidents are from the Ministry of Emergency Management; all the other data are from the National Bureau of Statistics.

In case of any differences between English translation and the original Chinese text, the Chinese edition shall prevail.